Media Law in Lithuania

Media Law in Lithuania

Ioannis Iglezakis

This book was originally published as a monograph in the International Encyclopaedia of Laws/Media Law.

Founding Editor: Roger Blanpain
General Editor: Frank Hendrickx
Volume Editors: Peggy Valcke & Eva Lievens

Wolters Kluwer

Published by:
Kluwer Law International B.V.
PO Box 316
2400 AH Alphen aan den Rijn
The Netherlands
E-mail: lrs-sales@wolterskluwer.com
Website: www.wolterskluwer.com/en/solutions/kluwerlawinternational

Sold and distributed by:
Wolters Kluwer Legal & Regulatory U.S.
7201 McKinney Circle
Frederick, MD 21704
United States of America
E-mail: customer.service@wolterskluwer.com

ISBN 978-94-035-4995-8

e-Book: ISBN 978-94-035-4695-7
web-PDF: ISBN 978-94-035-4705-3

The Authors

Simona Drukteinienė is currently Professor of Private Law at the Mykolas Romeris Law School of Mykolas Romeris University, Vilnius. She studied law at Vilnius University and in 2002, obtained a Master of Laws. She completed and defended her thesis on public liability at Mykolas Romeris University in 2008. Her spheres of interest include tort law, contract law, public liability and personality rights issues. Simona Drukteinienė is also a practicing lawyer and recommended arbitrator of the Vilnius Court of Commercial Arbitration. Simona Drukteinienė since 2010 participates in the annual European tort law project organized by the European Centre of Tort and Insurance Law (ECTIL) together with the Institute for European Tort Law, as well as in other projects on various specific issues of tort law organized by the Institute for European Tort Law. Since May 2017, Simona Drukteinienė has been appointed by the Minister of Justice as a member of the committee of the supervision of the Civil Code of the Republic of Lithuania. Simona Drukteinienė constantly delivers lectures and seminars to the members of the Lithuanian Bar Association and Lithuanian judges as well as other legal practitioners on various issues of tort law and contractual liability. She is also the partner and the head of the litigation department of Law Firm WALLESS.

Solveiga Vilčinskaitė (Palevičienė) is currently Professor of Private Law at the Mykolas Romeris Law School of Mykolas Romeris University, Vilnius. She has been teaching Contract Law, Investment Law, and Comparative Tort law at the University since 2003. She completed and defended her thesis on non-pecuniary damage at Mykolas Romeris University in 2008. Solveiga Vilčinskaitė (Palevičienė) has been participating in various research programmes on comparative tort law, such as the Digest of European Tort Law on Damage organized by the Institute for European Tort Law. Solveiga (Palevičienė) is also the managing partner and the head of the Legal Litigation and Arbitration Department at Glimstedt law firm. Her practice covers a wide range of corporate and commercial litigation and arbitration at both the domestic and international levels. Solveiga Vilčinskaitė (Palevičienė) has been included in the list of recommended arbitrators of the Vilnius Court of Commercial

Arbitration and has been designated to the ICSID (International Centre for Settlement of Investment Disputes) Panel of Arbitrators by the Lithuanian Government.

Table of Contents

List of Abbreviations

Civil code	Civil Code of the Republic of Lithuania
Commission	The Commission of Ethics of Lithuanian Journalists and Publishers
Constitution	Constitution of the Republic of Lithuania
Constitutional Court	Constitutional Court of the Republic of Lithuania
CRA	Communications Regulatory Authority of the Republic of Lithuania
Criminal code	Criminal Code of the Republic of Lithuania
DEPI	Republic of Lithuania Law on the Protection of Minors against the Detrimental Effect of Public Information
ECHR	European Court of Human Rights
Ethics Code	Code of Ethics of Lithuanian Journalists and Publishers
LEC	Republic of Lithuania Law on Electronic Communications
LNRT	Republic of Lithuania Law on the National Radio and Television
LPIP	Republic of Lithuania Law on the Provision of Information to the Public
LRT	Lithuanian National Radio and Television
LRTC	Lithuanian Radio and Television Commission
LRTK	Radio and Television Commission of Lithunia
SAC	Supreme Administrative Court of Lithuania
Seimas	Parliament of the Republic of Lithuania
VIRSIS	Information system for recording data of participants in public information producers and multipliers

List of Abbreviations

General Introduction

§1. General Background of the Country

I. Political System

1. According to the Constitution of the Republic of Lithuania[1] (hereinafter 'the Constitution') adopted in 1992 at the referendum of Lithuanian citizens, Lithuania is an independent democratic republic (Article 1) with a multi-party parliament. The form of governing is a parliamentary republic. The supreme legislative power is vested in the Seimas (Parliament), consisting of 141 members elected for a term of four years based on universal, equal and direct vote. The powers of the Seimas are defined by the Constitution and the laws of Lithuania. The President of Lithuania is elected for a five-year term, based on universal, equal and direct vote. The President represents the State of Lithuania and performs the functions prescribed to them by the Constitution and other laws. The supreme executive power rests with the Prime Minister who is appointed by the President and the Parliament.

2. Since 2004, Lithuania is an active member of both the European Union and the North Atlantic Treaty Organization. Lithuania's membership in international organizations is based upon the provision outlined in the Constitution (Article 135): 'to guarantee the security and independence of the country, the welfare of the citizens and their fundamental rights and liberties'.

II. Legal Systems

The primacy of Legislation and its Codification

3. Since Lithuania is a civil law country, its statutory law is of primary importance. As in all jurisdictions embedded in the civil law tradition, Lithuanian statutory law comprises a strict hierarchical system wherein all types of legal acts have their particular position depending on their legal power. On top of this hierarchy stands the Constitution. Its supremacy is enshrined in the Constitution itself. Article 7 of the Constitution states that any law or other act that contradicts the Constitution shall be invalid. Below in the hierarchy are situated Constitutional laws (e.g.,

1. Official gazette, 1992, No. 33-1014.

Civil Code, Penal Code, etc.) and legal acts implementing laws (e.g., resolutions of the Seimas and the Government, Presidential decrees, orders and acts of other governmental institutions and municipal authorities). Each one is legally subordinate to the preceding one in the sense that a legal act must not contradict another legal act of a higher legal power.

4. In Lithuania, many areas of substantial and procedural law are codified. The Civil Code of the Republic of Lithuania (hereinafter 'the Civil Code') encompasses company law, family law, the law of succession, and the law on obligations (paragraph 41). Legal matters related to employment are regulated by the Labour Code. Also, the Criminal Code regulates issues of penal law. Procedural norms are situated in the Code of Civil Procedure and the Code of Criminal Procedure. Administrative law regulates the status and competence of public administration entities, their mutual relations, and the relations with public and private law entities. It is also divided into two branches – general administrative law (lays down general principles) and special administrative law (norms, that cover specific areas of administrative law).

5. Even though statutory law in Lithuania has been historically considered a primary or supreme legal source in the vein of the civil law tradition, a decade ago judicial precedent has also acquired the status of a legal source. The basis of case law and its importance was formulated for the first time by the Constitutional Court of the Republic of Lithuania (hereinafter 'the Constitutional Court') in 2006.[2] According to this constitutional doctrine, the courts must follow rules and principles adopted in the previous case law when deciding subsequent cases with a similar factual background. This rule applies both vertically – judicial precedents bind courts of lower instances – and horizontally – judicial precedents bind the court itself that has adopted the precedent. Judicial precedents can be deviated from and new precedents can be formed only in exceptional circumstances.

6. According to Article 138 of the Constitution, international treaties ratified by the Seimas are a constituent part of the legal system of Lithuania. Law on International Treaties states that in case a ratified international treaty provides different legal rules than the ones established in the national law, an international treaty shall have the primacy of application (Article 11(2)).

Position of the Judiciary

7. The system of courts, their competence, the system of court organization, activity, administration, as well as the autonomy of courts, also the status of judges,

2. *See* the Ruling of the Constitutional Court of 28 Mar. 2006 'On the powers of the Constitutional Court to review its own decisions and dismiss the instituted legal proceedings, as well as on reviewing the financing of courts'. The texts of all rulings of the Constitutional Court are available in English at http://www.lrkt.lt.

their appointment, career, liability, and other issues related to the judicial activities are regulated by the Constitution, the Law on Courts[3] and other legal acts.

8. According to Article 109 of the Constitution, justice in Lithuania shall be administered only by courts. When administering justice, judges and courts shall be independent and shall obey only the law.

9. The court system of Lithuania is made up of courts of general jurisdiction and courts of special (administrative) jurisdiction.

10. The subsystem of courts of general competence consists of twelve district courts, five regional courts, the Lithuanian Court of Appeal and the Lithuanian Supreme Court.[4] These courts deal with civil and criminal cases. District courts also hear cases of administrative offenses coming within their jurisdiction by law. The regional courts, the Lithuanian Court of Appeal, and the Lithuanian Supreme Court have the Civil Division and the Criminal Division.

11. Concerning courts of special jurisdiction, there are five regional administrative courts and the Lithuanian Supreme Administrative Court. These courts hear disputes arising from administrative legal relations. Tort law cases arising out of damage caused by public authorities acting in their administrative capacity are also decided in the specialized administrative courts (paragraph 110).

12. Court decisions may be reviewed only by courts of the higher instance and only by the procedure prescribed by law.

13. Judges of district, regional and administrative courts are appointed by the President. Judges of the Lithuanian Court of Appeal are appointed by the President upon the assent of the Seimas and the Lithuanian Supreme Court justices are appointed by Seimas upon submission by the President. Judges serve in courts until the age of 65 unless there are grounds, established in the Constitution, for their dismissal or removal.

14. Lastly, the Constitutional Court is the institution that decides whether the laws and other acts of the Seimas are in conflict with the Constitution and whether the acts of the President and the Government are in conflict with the Constitution or laws. The Constitutional Court consists of nine justices, each appointed for a single nine-year term of office. Every three years, one-third of the Constitutional Court is reconstituted. The Seimas appoints an equal number of justices to the Constitutional Court, also in cases when the composition of the Court is being renewed, from the candidates presented by the President of the Republic, the Speaker of the Seimas, and the President of the Supreme Court.

3. No. IX-732, 24 Jan. 2002, Official gazette, 2002, No. 17-649 (20 Feb. 2002).
4. https://www.teismai.lt/lt/visuomenei-ir-ziniasklaidai/teismai-ir-teisejai/teismu-sistema/153.

III. Geography

15. The Republic of Lithuania is situated in Northern Europe on the south-eastern shore of the Baltic Sea. It is one of the three Baltic States (Lithuania, Latvia and Estonia), and the largest one. Lithuania shares its borders with Latvia in the north (558 km), Belarus in the southeast (653 km), Poland and the Kaliningrad Region of the Russian Federation in the southwest (104 km and 249 km, respectively). Its size is 65,300 sq. km, and it is larger than Belgium, Denmark, the Netherlands or Switzerland. Lithuania has approximately 99 km of sandy coastline. Lithuania has an ice-free port in Klaipėda, which is the most important and biggest Lithuanian transport hub, connecting sea, land and railway routes from East to West. The climate is midway between maritime and continental. In January the average daytime temperature is -3°C (27°F), rising in July to average +20°C (68°F).

IV. Population

16. At this moment, the population of Lithuania is 2,795,680 million.[5] Thus, the population density of this country is 42.8 people per square kilometre, ranking in at 165th in the world for population density.[6]

17. The last time an increase in permanent residents had been recorded was in 1991. The growth of the population was determined by the fact that 10,800 more people arrived in Lithuania than departed from it. The increase in the population is determined by the growing standard of living in Lithuania. More than half of the people who immigrated are Lithuanian citizens, the rest are mostly Ukrainians and Belarusians.

18. The five largest cities in Lithuania are Vilnius (550,834 residents) – which is also the capital of Lithuania, Kaunas (289,364), Klaipėda (149,116), Šiauliai (101,511) and Panevėžys (85,885).[7]

V. Presence of Minorities

19. National minorities in Lithuania are an integral part of the society, with long-term cultural ties to Lithuania.

20. The government of the Republic of Lithuania with the resolution of 2015 July 1, established the Department of National Minorities under the Government of

5. Data from Statistics Department of Lithuania. https://osp.stat.gov.lt/statistiniu-rodikliu-analize?hash=103cad31-9227-4990-90b0-8991b58af8e7#/.
6. *Ibid.*
7. Data from Statistics Department of Lithuania. https://osp.stat.gov.lt/lietuvos-gyventojai-2020/salies-gyventojai/miesto-ir-kaimo-gyventojai.

the Republic of Lithuania. It is an institution of the Government of the Republic of Lithuania that participates in the formation and implementation of the policy on national minorities.

21. On 15 January 2021, the Lithuanian department of statistics launched a new statistical survey on the nationality, mother tongue and religion of the population. During the process, residents were asked what is their nationality, what other languages do they know apart from their mother tongue, what religion do they profess. The last census took place in 2011. According to it, 154 nationalities are present in Lithuania's society and they also belonged to 59 different religious communities.[8]

VI. Social and Cultural Values

22. The concept of value is ambiguous and a changing, eternal topic of philosophical and old sociological debate. From the point of view of the social sciences, values are one of the main components of any culture, forming the basis of individuals' personal and collective identities, influencing people's daily social life, the formation, establishment, and functioning of social institutions, and the development of society. According to the statistics of 2008, scientists, philosophers, and sociologists,[9] Lithuanians consider the following life values most important: family, work, friends, religion and politics.

23. Article 38 of the Constitution states that 'the family is the foundation of society and the state'. The state protects and cares for the family, motherhood, fatherhood and childhood. The twentieth century in Western societies has been marked by significant demographic and value changes in family life. In terms of changes in matrimonial and procreative behaviour, the age of first marriage and first childbirth has risen quite sharply since the 1960s, the number of children in families has decreased, the number of divorces has increased, and new forms of partnership have been found. Due to modernization and individualization, important changes in values have taken place, which has also affected family life: the importance of equal opportunities and the freedom of human choice are increasingly emphasized. The aspirations for self-expression and self-realization were inevitably reflected in the relationships between family members, both spouses or partners, and between different generations of the family, changing the forms and quality of family life and the expectations associated with it. In post-communist societies in Eastern and Central Europe, these demographic and value changes took place at least a couple of decades later and are associated not only with the internal processes of social development but also with the adoption of Western values and ideas as examples of a more perfect society.[10]

8. Data from Statistics Department of Lithuania. https://osp.stat.gov.lt/gyventoju-ir-bustu-surasymai1.
9. Žiliukaitė R., Poviliūnas A., Savicka A., *Changes in values of Lithuanian society during the twenty years of independence:* Monograph 2016 of September 14, 18p.
10. Žiliukaitė R., Poviliūnas A., Savicka A., *Changes in values of Lithuanian society during the twenty years of independence:* Monograph 2016 of September 14, 24p.

24. The Constitution guarantees the social protection of employees. The Constitutional Court has noted that the state must create a system of social welfare that will help to maintain the dignity of the person and the living conditions. Article 48 of the Constitution declares that everyone is free to choose a job and business and has the right to have adequate, safe, and healthy working conditions, to receive fair pay for work and social security in the event of unemployment. Workers' professional, economic and social rights are protected by trade unions Article 50.[11] Workers also have the right to strike following the procedure laid down by law Article 51.[12] The State guarantees citizens the right to old-age and disability pensions, social assistance in cases of unemployment, sickness, widowhood, loss of a breadwinner, and other statutory cases Article 52.[13]

25. Taking into account the differences between the situation and opportunities of men and women in the labour market, in general, in Lithuanian society gender does not differentiate between evaluations of the importance of work as an essential activity of life, various aspects of work and values related to work ethic. In terms of the impact of age on the importance of work, the life-cycle effect is evident when work is most valued by active labour market participants. Age had such an effect on the concept of work and value orientations that younger people placed more emphasis on cognitive work values, cared more about working with pleasant co-workers and interesting work, and older people had a stronger work ethic. Perceptions of the work concept and ethics of people with different education also differ significantly, as less educated people perceive it in traditional categories of moral duty, and more educated people associate it with self-realization, personal growth, emphasizing cognitive work values and responsibilities. Thus, the phenomena typical of Western societies in Lithuania are only partially confirmed: unlike there, people of higher social status in Lithuania value work as important in their lives more than lower ones; however, as in the West, they more often associate the concept of work with self-realization and cognitive values.[14]

26. Regarding leisure time as a value for the Lithuanian population, it did not equal the importance of family or work, it grew insignificantly but steadily during the period 1990–2008, especially due to cohort changes: for younger people, leisure time is even more important than for older ones, and this reveals not only the influence of age on value orientations but also significant cohort differences. Urban residents value leisure time a little more than rural residents, and in this respect, the residents of the capital stand out the most. Concerning other demographic factors in the assessment of the importance of leisure time, such an unambiguous link is not detected. Although people with higher education are more likely to value leisure than others, they still prefer work in the face of a choice between work and leisure. Similarly, people who are more engaged in work are more likely to value leisure

---

11. Constitution of the Republic of Lithuania, 1992.
12. *Ibid.*
13. *Ibid.*
14. Žiliukaitė R., Poviliūnas A., Savicka A., *Changes in values of Lithuanian society during the twenty years of independence:* Monograph 2016 of September 14, 100 p.

than those who are not in paid employment. Moreover, people on higher incomes tend to value leisure much more than those on lower incomes, and the gap between groups at different ends of the income scale is huge. It is already a regularity here that people with higher incomes tend to agree less with the statement about the unconditional preference of work over leisure. Among the various aspects of leisure time, the importance of carefree leisure activities (relaxation, rest, socializing) dominates in the Lithuanian population, while serious leisure activities (which are related to the desire to learn something new and improve) ranked at the end of the list of priorities.[15]

27. Article 43 of the Constitution stipulates that 'there is no state religion in Lithuania'. As mentioned before, the latest data from the Department of Statistics for 2011, 154 nationalities living in Lithuania belong to 59 different religious communities.[16] Having that in mind, the Catholic church is still quite influential and active in social and political debates. Statistics reveal that Lithuania is one of the European societies with a relatively strong religious identity and that many European countries are more secularized in terms of individual religiosity (e.g., Poland, Ireland, Slovakia), the gap between them is as great as with many societies more affected by processes of secularization (e.g., Denmark, Iceland, Finland).[17]

28. According to Article 29 of the Constitution, human rights cannot be restricted and no privileges shall be granted based on sex, race, nationality, language, origin, social status, belief or opinion. Furthermore, the freedom to express convictions and disseminate information is incompatible with incitement to hatred, violence and discrimination, defamation and disinformation. Despite what is officially written in the Constitution and laws, Lithuania can be called a country with one of the weakest civil societies in Europe.[18] Whatever aspect of the civic attitude of the population we take – trust in the citizens of the country, solidarity with socially excluded groups, tolerance for people with different lifestyles, support for the political community, democratic principles, functioning and institutions, civic activism – Lithuania's position in comparison with other countries, in the context of Eastern Europe, testifies to the fact that our society is severely damaged not only by political but also by social alienation. Civil society is strong in those societies which focus children's values more on the qualities of the individual that foster interpersonal communication and cooperation from a young age: tolerance and respect for the other person, selflessness, and a sense of responsibility. The population of Lithuania, as well as the population of many other post-communist countries of Eastern and Central Europe, attaches much less importance to such characteristics than to the characteristics of a person, which give independence and autonomy from others, i.e., those qualities that reduce the need for collaboration with other people.

15. Žiliukaitė R., Poviliūnas A., Savicka A., *Changes in values of Lithuanian society during the twenty years of independence:* Monograph 2016 of September 14, 133 p.
16. Data from Statistics Department of Lithuania. https://osp.stat.gov.lt/gyventoju-ir-bustu-surasymai1.
17. Žiliukaitė R., Poviliūnas A., Savicka A., *Changes in values of Lithuanian society during the twenty years of independence:* Monograph 2016 of September 14, 162 p.
18. Žiliukaitė R., Poviliūnas A., Savicka A., *Changes in values of Lithuanian society during the twenty years of independence:* Monograph 2016 of September 14, 217–218p.

This feature of the Lithuanian culture is worth keeping in mind when trying to understand not only the economic but also the cultural preconditions for the strengthening of the country's civil society.[19]

§2. The Media Landscape

I. Overview of Media Markets and Main Actors

29. According to the statistics, there are 515 printed press sources, 44 television channels, 437 websites, 57 radio channels/companies, 3 news agencies (AINA, BNS, Elta) and 43 politicians and civil servants that are active in covering news and other information in Lithuania.[20]

30. Television. Television in Lithuania is at the hands of private companies (MG Baltic, Providence Equity Partners), that indirectly manage multiple channels at once, together with some radio stations and news websites. Although there is an exception where one television entity (Lithuanian National Radio and Television (LRT)) is a state-owned public body, that manages over a few television channels as well as radio stations.

31. Radio stations. There are two biggest rivalling, private companies in Lithuania ('M-1' and 'Radiocentras'). Although, as stated above, there is a radio station that is state-owned, and there are exceptions where a state can interfere with what is being broadcasted, the market is occupied by private companies.

32. Speaking of media, websites and press, there are no ways to find each and everyone's shareholders, therefore – only the biggest companies choose to be transparent (DELFI, 15min, Lrytas), about their interests and shareholders. Accordingly, those companies, adapted to Lithuania's market, are the ones that dominate it.

33. To conclude, at the moment the media representatives declare their interests voluntarily, the law in Lithuania compared to other West European countries does not provide the best application of the principle of transparency. Although it is mandatory for the owners and shareholders, if they hold more than 10% shares, according to the law on Provision of Information to the Public of the Republic of Lithuania, Articles 22 (3), 24 (1), of media groups, to publicly declare in the public register what other businesses do they have, who are the owners of those businesses, it is not transparent enough. Public interests still clash with private business pursuits.

19. *Ibid.*
20. https://stirna.info/.

II. Broadcasting Infrastructure

34. Radio, television broadcasting activities and/or retransmission activities are licensed in the Republic of Lithuania using the radio frequencies provided for in the Radio Frequency Allocation Plan for radio and television broadcasting.

35. In Lithuania, smart TV (provided via the Internet) is the most popular, although there are other alternatives to satellite and terrestrial television (terrestrial, satellite).[21] The radio usually broadcasts on radio waves and is most often listened to in the car, although the radio can also be listened to online.

36. Licenses for broadcasting and retransmission of content shall be issued only to legal persons and entities established in the States of the European Economic Area and without legal personality.[22] It can also be issued to branches of such legal persons and entities established in the Republic of Lithuania and other States of the European Economic Area without legal personality.[23] In case circumstances laid down in the Law on Provision of Information to the Public of the Republic of Lithuania are not met, the Lithuanian Radio and Television Commission (LRTC) must refuse to issue a broadcasting or retransmission license (paragraphs 181–189).

III. Technological and Economic Developments on the Media Markets

37. It is considered, that Lithuanian Internet media strives to make maximum use of artificial intelligence solutions that ensure independent and effective dissemination of advertising. Lithuanian media is preparing for a new step – to apply foreign-proven artificial intelligence algorithms, which would facilitate the work of editorial offices in preparing content, and help readers to offer what is most interesting to them.[24] According to a report from the Internet Media Association, this is an innovation, but trends suggest that there will be more such solutions in the future, as they are convenient, save time and allow more of them to prepare serious content.

38. A. Marcinkus, the head of the Lithuanian Internet Media Association, says that in the digital world, everything that facilitates work is exploited.[25] Artificial

21. https://www.fastlink.lt/en/televizijos-rusys.
22. Republic of Lithuania law on licensing rules for broadcasting activities and retrospected content, Art. 8.
23. LPIP Art. 2.9.
24. Lithuanian artificial intelligence strategy – https://eimin.lrv.lt/uploads/eimin/documents/files/DI_strategija_ENG(1).pdf.
25. Dirbtinis intelektas žengia į interneto žiniasklaidą – M360 (delfi.lt).

intelligence and the tools that come with it are one of the hottest trends in the market. Properly applied artificial intelligence algorithms allow robotic systems to prepare template news, for example, from sports matches, various competitions, Olympiads. Their prepared texts also travel to news portals and are visible in the stream.[26]

39. Moreover, the method of combining has been proven very effective in Lithuania. Media convergence – merging different types of mass media such as Traditional media, Print Media, Broadcast media, New Media and the Internet through digital media platforms such as smartphones, online radio, apps, news websites, E-books is an advantageous Media market means to reach as many users as possible. Moreover, combining future prospects of digital algorithms creates an opportunity to filtrate information instantly and to adapt specific news and advertisements to every user.[27]

40. Lastly, the economic strength of the media is also one of the conditions for freedom of expression – the best interest of the public. If specific media or the whole system is constrained, there is a lack of capacity to create independent content. Of course, freedom does not in itself guarantee quality content. As mentioned before, some media organizations in Lithuania have economic interests in other areas. In this case, it is precisely because of economic interests that the media they control cannot be completely free (paragraph 33).

§3. Sources of Media Law

41. The basis of media law is the Constitution of Lithuania. The main provisions of public information entrenched in the Constitution are: human rights and freedoms are innate (Article 18); human dignity is protected by law (Article 21); the private life of a person is inviolable (Article 22); a person has the right to possess and freely express beliefs (Article 25); a person, while exercising his rights and exercising his freedoms, must observe the Constitution and laws and not restrict the rights and freedoms of other people (Article 28); censorship of mass information is prohibited; state, political parties, political and public organisations, other institutions or persons may not monopolise the mass media (Article 44).

42. The main codified acts of law in Lithuania are the Civil Code, Criminal Code, and Administrative laws (Code of Administrative Offences, Law on administrative proceedings). The Civil Code in regards to media law covers principles of fairness, transparency, equal rights, etc. As well as it is needed if a person is being sued for civil liability, or any other dispute, that is not directly governed by the Law on Provision of Information to the Public of the Republic of Lithuania. The same goes if there was a criminal or administrative offence.

26. *Ibid.*
27. Mapping digital media – https://www.opensocietyfoundations.org/uploads/2de7585c-1048-404a-bee2-3ea025e3722c/mapping-digital-media-lithuania-20110923.pdf pp. 41–46.

43. One of the most important acts of law, on public informing, is the Law on the Provision of Information to the Public (LPIP). The LPIP regulates the functioning of free and responsible media in the country and the legitimacy of the dissemination of public information. Naturally, to achieve a functioning and viable model of a democratic society, the LPIP establishes the self-regulation of the media system itself. Chapter V of the LPIP regulates the activities of producers and disseminators of public information and establishes the competencies of self-regulatory institutions. According to Meškauskaitė L. this law falls within the category of complex legislation because it regulates legal relationships whose boundaries cannot be formalized and covers a very wide range of them, from one person's private life to addressing the basic issues of public awareness.[28] It is also this law that implements the legislation of the European Union.[29]

44. Other laws include the Code of Ethics for Journalists and Publishers (hereinafter 'Ethics commission') which regulates main questions of ethics, Republic of Lithuania Law on the National Radio and Television (LNRT), the Law on Advertising, Republic of Lithuania Law on Electronic Communications (LEC) and other administrative laws and regulations.

---

28. Liudvika Meškauskaitė, *Media Law*, 2nd ed., Vilnius: Centre of Registers, 2018, 53.
29. 3 Oct. 1989 Council Directive 89/552/EEC on the coordination of certain provisions laid down by law, regulation or administrative action in Member States concerning the pursuit of television broadcasting activities (OJ 2004, Special Edition, Chapter 6, Volume 1, p. 224); 30 Jun. 1997 Directive 97/36/EC of the European Parliament and of the Council amending Council Directive 89/552/EEC on the coordination of certain provisions laid down by law, regulation or administrative action in Member States concerning the pursuit of television broadcasting activities (OJ 2004, Special Edition, Chapter 6) 2, p. 321); 20 Jul. 1998 Directive 98/48/EC of the European Parliament and of the Council amending Directive 98/34/EC laying down a procedure for the provision of information in the field of technical standards and regulations (OJ 2004, Special Edition, Chapter 13, Volume 21, p. 8); 27 Oct. 2004 Regulation (EC) No. 1049/2001 of the European Parliament and of the Council 2006/2004 on cooperation between national authorities responsible for the enforcement of consumer protection laws (OC 2004 L 364, p. 1).

Part I. Freedom of Speech

Chapter 1. The Constitutional Protection of Press and Broadcasting Freedoms in Lithuania

45. After the restoration of the independence of the Republic of Lithuania,[30] the constitutional protection of the free and independent media in Lithuania was enshrined in the core of Lithuanian Law – the Constitution.[31] When addressing the issue of the status of the Radio and Television of Lithuania in the independent restored State of Lithuania, the Constitutional Court of the Republic of Lithuania stressed that the laws lay down and protect not only freedom of information,[32] in general, but also freedom of means of mass media as the expression of freedom of information.[33]

46. The constitutional and inherent right of every human being to information is broad in its content. According to the provisions of Article 25 of the Constitution, the constitutional basis of freedom of expression includes:

(1) the right to have one's convictions and express them freely;
(2) the right to seek, receive and impart information and ideas;
(3) the prohibition to limit one's freedom to express convictions, to receive and impart information otherwise than by law and only if this is necessary to protect the health, honour and dignity, private life, and morals of others, or to defend the constitutional order;
(4) the mandatory provision on the incompatibility of freedom to express convictions and to impart information with criminal actions (i.e. incitement of national, racial, religious, or social hatred, violence and discrimination, defamation and disinformation);
(5) the citizen's right to receive, according to the procedure established by law, any information concerning them that is held by State institutions.

30. The independence of the Republic of Lithuania was restored on 11 Mar. 1990.
31. Official gazette, 1992, No. 33-1014.
32. According to the case law of the Constitutional Court of the Republic of Lithuania, the concepts of 'freedom of information' and 'freedom of expression' are used as synonyms.
33. Ruling of the Constitutional Court of the Republic of Lithuania of 20 Apr. 1995. The texts of all rulings of the Constitutional Court are available in English at http://www.lrkt.lt.

47. The constitutional doctrine recognizes[34] that the free and universal exchange of information and its unrestricted dissemination are particularly important factors in democratic processes which ensure not only the formation of individual opinion and subjective convictions but also that of group views, including political, as well as that of the whole nation's will.

48. The Constitution does not permit the establishment of any such legal regulation whereby, by entrenching the guarantees of implementation of freedom of information, preconditions would be created to violate other constitutional values and their balance.[35] Therefore, limitations on freedom of information are established and the activity of mass media is regulated by national laws.[36] However, the limitations of freedom of information and the regulation of means of mass media must not violate pluralism – a principle of a democratic society. This is guaranteed by a prohibition against the monopolization of means of mass media and information censorship, as well as by other legal means.[37]

49. Greater demands are raised for radio and television than for other means of mass media for their especially great influence upon the broad audience also because the technical possibilities of radio and television broadcasting are not limitless.[38] The same basic principles of the job of the transmitter putting on the air – impartiality and pluralism – are valid for both private and public or State radio and television broadcasters.

34. Ruling of the Constitutional Court of the Republic of Lithuania of 13 Feb. 1997.
35. Ruling of the Constitutional Court of the Republic of Lithuania of 15 May 2007.
36. Ruling of the Constitutional Court of the Republic of Lithuania of 20 Apr. 1995.
37. *Ibid.*
38. *Ibid.*

Chapter 2. The Conditions for Public Authorities to Restrict Freedom of Speech

50. The constitutional doctrine of the Republic of Lithuania states that the principle of recognition of the inherent nature of human rights and freedoms does not exclude the fact that the implementation of human rights and freedoms may be restricted.[39] Recognizing that like other constitutional rights and freedoms, freedom of expression is not absolute and in certain cases, the government may limit freedom of expression. That is why it is necessary to determine in which cases the limitation of freedom of expression is a fair and reasonable action.

51. Lithuanian case law[40] notes that any restrictions on freedom of information must be based on the same constitutional criteria as restrictions on other fundamental human rights and freedoms.

52. Limitation of freedom of expression is fair and reasonable if the following constitutional conditions are followed:[41]

(1) a limitation is necessary for a democratic society;
(2) the purpose of a limitation is to protect the rights and freedoms of others and values entrenched in the Constitution, as well as the constitutionally important objectives;
(3) a limitation does not deny the nature and essence of the rights and freedoms;
(4) the constitutional principle of proportionality is followed.

53. Article 25 paragraph 4 of the Constitution *expressis verbis* lays down the grounds[42] when limitations of freedom of expression which are established by law are fair and reasonable (if it is based on criminal activities – incitement to national, racial, religious hatred, violence and discrimination, defamations and misinformation). The same article directly stipulates that (1) this is necessary to protect the health, honour and dignity, private life, and morals of a human being or (2) to defend the constitutional order. However, when setting legal restrictions and liability for violations of law, one must pay heed to the requirement of reasonableness.[43]

54. The constitutional rules which lay down and limit freedom of speech are implemented in the national legal acts in order to achieve a number of protection

39. Ruling of the Constitutional Court of the Republic of Lithuania of 29 December 2004.
40. Supreme Administrative Court of Lithuania, 23 Jul. 2020, Case No. eA-1639-520/2020.
41. Ruling of the Constitutional Court of the Republic of Lithuania of 29 December 2004.
42. The grounds in the Lithuanian legal framework reflect the objectives of limitation of freedom of expression as laid down in Art. 10 para. 2 of the European Convention on Human Rights. The identical constitutional grounds of limitation of freedom of expression are laid down in Art. 4 para. 1 of the Republic of Lithuania Law on the Provision of Information to the Public (LPIP).
43. Rulings of the Constitutional Court of the Republic of Lithuania of 13 December 2004 and 29 Sep. 2005.

purposes. For example, one of the fundamental values justifying a limitation of freedom of expression is the protection of information covered by state secrecy. Information covered by state secrecy includes state, commercial, professional and technological secrets.[44]

55. Since disclosure or loss of such information may cause damage to the national interests therefore the sovereignty of the State, this constitutional protection is further implemented by additional laws (paragraph 104).

44. Ruling of the Constitutional Court of the Republic of Lithuania of 19 December 1996.

Part II. Regulation of Print Media

Chapter 1. The Journalists' Profession

56. The essence of journalistic activity is the realization of freedom of expression (freedom of information, under the Republic of Lithuania Law on the Provision of Information to the Public (LPIP),[45] guaranteed by the Constitution. While regulating the activities, rights, obligations and liability of journalists, the State lays down the limits of journalists' freedom of lawful activities.

57. In Lithuania, the concept of journalist *expressis verbis* is defined in Article 2(72) of the LPIP, which states that 'Journalist' means a natural person who, on a professional basis, collects, prepares and presents material to the producer and/or disseminator of public information under a contract with him and/or is a member of a professional journalists' association. However, since 2009 courts are presenting a wider perspective on the concept of a journalist[46] than the one provided by the law. Since 2009, the Supreme Administrative Court of Lithuania (SAC) has clarified that in Lithuania any natural or legal person who collects information regularly or on a professional basis and disseminates it to society through any means of media is considered a journalist.[47]

58. It is important to note that journalists and producers of public information can be the same person. This is not regulated by the LPIP, but this circumstance is acknowledged by Lithuanian courts. Article 2(72) must be interpreted as meaning that in cases, when the producer of public information and the person who, on a professional basis, collects and prepares material for the producer of public information is the same natural person, the agreement between him/her and the producer of public information would be meaningless, to recognize this person as a journalist, because it is an agreement where two parties are the same party. And in addition to that, if the law would forbid that a journalist could not be the same person as the producer of public information, it would be unlawful according to the Constitutional norm, which guarantees the right to choose a job or a business freely Article

45. The jurisprudence of the Constitutional Court of the Republic of Lithuania uses the concept of 'freedom of expression' whereas the LPIP uses the concept of 'freedom of information'. Freedom of information includes all media *inter alia* print media. Hereinafter, the concepts 'freedom of expression' and 'freedom of information' will be used as synonyms in so far as the specific context does not require the use of a specific concept.
46. Supreme Administrative Court of Lithuania, 20 Apr. 2009, Case No. A-444-70/2009.
47. *Ibid.*

48(1). In such cases, to decide whether the person complies with the characteristics of a journalist, it is sufficient to determine whether the natural person collects, prepares and provides material on a professional basis (paragraphs 69–72) to be used by himself while acting as producer of public information.

59. The Lithuanian national legal regulation does not lay down any specific definitions relating to the restriction of the right to engage in journalistic activity or, in other words, to be a journalist (e.g., no specific requirements are set at the state level, no journalistic education is required, no license or permit for professional activity is necessary, there is no requirement for impeccable reputation, and it is not obligatory to work in an editorial office under an employment contract).

60. Interpretation of the concept of 'journalist' is broad in Lithuania and is based on the free and unhindered development of journalistic activity which is an integral part of freedom of expression and the right of the public to be informed about the significant events of public life.[48]

61. For example, Lithuanian case law[49] clarifies that bloggers may be treated in the same way as journalists and for accreditation to public authorities, but must prove, to the accrediting authority that their functions are in principle equivalent to those of accredited journalists. They should comply as far as possible, given their specific status, the obligations that are imposed on natural persons and journalists by public information producers, as well as other requirements set by the accrediting bodies (professionalism, purpose and regular preparation and publication of public information on the activities of the accrediting body, internal procedures, etc.).

62. The case law of the Lithuanian courts upholds the position[50] that in order to determine whether a person meets the characteristics of a journalist, it is sufficient to determine whether a natural person is engaged in the collection, production and provision of material that is used by him as the producer of public information in a way that relates to a profession or a career.

63. Moreover, it should be mentioned that Lithuania is attributed to modern democracies as the concept of 'the media' includes not only the traditional (e.g., press, television, radio, etc.) but also modern, online media, though not directly regulated. It was already in 2009 when the Supreme Administrative Court of Lithuania[51] clarified that although our legal acts do not regulate the concept of Internet blogs or the status of their managers (owners), in the light of the specific nature of activities performed by Internet bloggers. As mentioned before, in certain circumstances, an Internet blogger is also considered and recognized as a journalist, that is why the Internet blog is treated as media.

48. Supreme Administrative Court of Lithuania, 20 Apr. 2009, Case No. A-444-70/2009.
49. *Ibid.*
50. *Ibid.*
51. *Ibid.*

64. Thus, if the court decides in a particular case that based on the nature of the public information functions a person falls within the concept of a journalist, such person is subject to the provisions of and *inter alia* the liability under the CC, the LPIP and the Code of Ethics of Lithuanian Journalists and Publishers (hereinafter 'Ethics code').

Chapter 2. Journalists' Rights

§1. Role of Journalists as 'Watch-Dogs' of Society

65. It is undeniable that journalists are referred to as 'watch-dogs' – alerting the public about the possible threats and violations of the law. Journalists' hands play an important function in political communication to society.[52] Lithuania is not an exception since the duty to inform the public in the area of investigative journalism about the significant political and public issues stems from the constitutional right to freedom of expression.[53] The duties of the journalist as a professional in the provision of information are laid down in Articles 41–44 of the LPIP.

66. It has to be admitted that it occurred only a few years ago that individual journalists started speaking more loudly about their work in the area of investigative journalism. Nevertheless, investigative journalism is rather weak in the country. In general, investigative journalism is a strong tool to make any governmental or major public establishment transparent – to expose corruption, hold individuals and institutions accountable for misusing their public power, uncovering the truth to the public. This role that the media plays as a watchdog is indispensable for democracy. Unfortunately, in Lithuania, it is not fortified, especially after the last global economic crisis hit the media, editors state that it is too expensive to operate with investigative journalism, rather more profitable to update on fast news (quantity over quality).[54]

67. Moreover, because investigative journalists tend to comment on public, and political figures, that is why there is always a clash between these powers. The most recent threat to press freedom was made by several attempts (paragraphs 109, 110) of the ruling political party (Farmers and Greens Union). In order to gain political control, a special parliamentary committee was established to investigate the financial transparency of the public service media LRT.[55] As expected, Constitutional Court stated[56] that the true nature of those actions was to put political pressure on journalists and to weaken the public broadcaster, which is an unlawful act. To explain, the lack of transparency in news outlets is clear (paragraph 33), but even so, it does not justify the establishment of a parliamentary commission, which consists of politicians, who are not the experts on public service media on any grounds.

---

52. Jurgita Matačinskaitė 'Žurnalisto kompetencijos ir gebėjimai šiandienos žiniasklaidoje' (*Journalist's Competences and Skills in Modern Media*), *Scientific Journal (Communication and Information)*, 2010 No. 3, at 117. https://www.zurnalai.vu.lt/zurnalistikos-tyrimai/article/view/63/10403.
53. Article 25 para. 2 of the Constitution of the Republic of Lithuania.
54. https://www.opensocietyfoundations.org/uploads/2de7585c-1048-404a-bee2-3ea025e3722c/mapping-digital-media-lithuania-20110923.pdf pp. 46–47.
55. https://www.lrt.lt/en/news-in-english/19/1165828/lithuania-sees-attempts-against-freedom-of-expression-report.
56. Ruling of the Constitutional Court of the Republic of Lithuania of 16 May 2019.

§2. JOURNALISTS' INDEPENDENCE

68. The independence of journalists in Lithuania is guaranteed by Article 10 of LPIP which directly prohibits censorship.[57]

69. The Ethics Code[58] has been adopted on a basis of the principle of fundamental independence of journalistic activity and its preamble declares that independence, fairness and objectivity of a journalist form the basis for journalist reliability. The independence can also be seen by the fact it was not Seimas that adopted this act, but in fact, the journalist ethics Inspector. The integrity and the legal power of this act are not on equal grounds with other fundamental codes – such as the Civil Code or the Criminal Code, it is more of an internal legal act for verified journalists. If violated, there would be no basis to use civil, administrative or criminal liability directly.

70. Article 24(2) of the Ethics Code notifies that journalist has a right to refuse a task given by the producer of public information or by his superior if this task conflicts with state laws, the ethics of the journalist or his beliefs. Article 27 of the Ethics Code also imposes a mandatory ban on accepting gifts, paid travel, paid leave and other persuasions that may be detrimental to their independence. In addition, in all cases, the journalist has to inform society about any support received except the salary paid or support given by the producer of public information with whom the journalist has employment or creative relationship.

71. However, it has to be admitted that the independence of the journalist and transparency of his activities depend only on the journalist himself, as the courts have stated – even the Internet bloggers are considered journalists. Therefore, from the legal point of view, the independence of the journalist's activities must be understood not only as a privilege granted by law but also as an obligation that is assessed in the context of the ethics of journalism.

72. According to Article 25 of the Lithuanian Code of Ethics for Journalists and Publishers, a journalist shall not be entitled to assume any other obligations, except for professional obligations to the producer of public information, in the course of his or her activities.

57. Article 10 of LPIP lays down that 'censorship of public information is prohibited in the Republic of Lithuania. Any actions whereby an attempt is made to control the content of information to be published in the media before its publication, with the exception of cases provided for by law, are prohibited.'
58. Lietuvos žurnalistų ir leidėjų etikos kodeksas (2005). Informaciniai pranešimai, No. 47-435.

§3. PROTECTION OF JOURNALISTIC SOURCES

73. The independence of journalists is directly associated with their other rights, i.e., protection of the source of information (Article 8 of the LPIP). The legal protection of the source of information enables the journalist to guarantee the anonymity of the source of information.

74. The Constitutional Court[59] has ruled that although protection of the source of information is not absolute, in extraordinary cases the court has the right to decide whether a journalist must disclose the source of information. This decision can be applied only if all other means of disclosure of the source of information have been exhausted. Therefore, disclosure of the source of information should be perceived as the *ultima ratio* means and should be justified only if it is necessary to protect much more significant interests protected by the Constitution.

75. The said clarification by the Constitutional Court has been implemented in Article 8 paragraph 2 of the LPIP which lays down that a journalist may be ordered to disclose the source of information only by a reasoned decision of the court. However, for the court to order disclosure of the source of information it is necessary to establish that:

(1) This is necessary for vitally important or otherwise significant public interests;
(2) Disclosure of the source of information will ensure the protection of persons' constitutional rights and freedoms;
(3) This would ensure the administration of justice;
(4) It is impossible to disclose the source of information by any other means or where such means have already been exhausted.
(5) As a last resort, following the rules laid down in the Code of Criminal Procedure of the Republic of Lithuania and to disclose the source of information, a search or seizure may be carried out at the journalist's place of work, residential and auxiliary premises or vehicle.[60] However, this is seen as a particularly extreme and exceptional measure which is justified only to protect the public interest and only when all other possibilities of disclosure of the source of information have been exhausted.

59. Ruling of the Constitutional Court of the Republic of Lithuania of 23 Oct. 2002.
60. Article 8 para. 3 of the LPIP.

Chapter 3. Journalists' Liability

§1. General Information on the Liability System

76. The Lithuanian legal regulation does not contain any special rules on the liability of a journalist, compared to any other citizen.

77. Under Lithuanian law, for the violation of legal provisions, a journalist may be brought to civil liability (in the form of compensation of damages and payment of penalties), administrative liability and criminal liability.

I. Civil Liability

78. Disputes arising from violations of non-property rights in the media in the course of the provision of information to the public are generally settled by civil law.

79. Notwithstanding the removal of criminal liability for insult, a person's public or non-public humiliation remains delict, i.e. an act contrary to the law that undermines a person's honour and dignity.[61] The national case law upholds the position that 'information that another person has committed a crime is of the offensive, humiliating nature in itself, results in the acknowledgement of the right to claim compensation of non-pecuniary damage'.[62] That means, it does not matter if the information is correct or not, just the fact of such information published, without stating the true source of information,[63] can result in civil liability for the journalist or the publishing company. In addition, the court can decide whether the non-pecuniary damage is proportional compared to the damage made to the person's reputation by slander and defamatory statements. Contrary to the basis of civil liability is that Article 154 of the Criminal Code can be adapted, when a person stating certain defamatory facts about another in public, knows that the information is incorrect, but still chooses to publish it on purpose.

80. In addition to this, in Lithuania, the media and the person who has performed unlawful actions may be brought to civil liability for the violation of freedom of expression and other non-property rights of others. For example, the media and the person can be brought to civil liability for the violation of the natural person's honour and dignity, professional reputation of the legal entity, right to one's image and inviolability of private life.

61. Article 2.24 of the Civil Code of the Republic of Lithuania: 'Explanatory Letter concerning the Draft Law on the Amendment of Article 2.24 of the Civil Code of the Republic of Lithuania'. https://e-seimas.lrs.lt/rs/legalact/TAK/0cdc2a70683c11e5b316b7e07d98304b/.
62. Supreme Court of Lithuania, 18 December 2012, Case No. 2K-638/2012.
63. Article 54 of the Provision of information made to the public of the Republic of Lithuania.

81. There may be cases where a journalist is exempted from liability. In the cases of violation of a person's honour and dignity, a journalist who has disseminated untrue data may be exempted from civil liability under the following conditions: (1) the data were announced in respect of a public person or his official or public activities; (2) the journalist proves that they acted in good faith; and (3) the aim was to make the person and his activities known to the public.[64]

II. Administrative Liability

82. According to the Code of Administrative Offences of the Republic of Lithuania,[65] only a broadcaster of radio or television programs, manager, or any other responsible person of the providers of on-demand audiovisual public information services may be a subject of administrative liability in the area of provision of information to the public.

83. Generally, administrative liability may be applied for:

- detrimental effect on the development of minors for the violation of requirements of marking and/or dissemination of public information;[66]
- non-compliance with the requirements of dissemination of political advertising;[67]
- violation of the procedure of provision and public announcement of data on the participants of legal entities who are publishers of local, regional and national newspapers and magazines or managers of the information society media;[68]
- violation of the requirements of television advertising, teleshopping, products placement, advertising in radio programs, audiovisual commercial communications and support of audiovisual media services, radio programs and/or individual programs;[69]
- showing television and radio programs, cinematographic films, without the translation to the state language;[70]
- distribution or demonstration of Nazi or communist symbols;[71]
- refusal to provide information to representatives of media or obstructing journalists in the exercise of their professional duties[72] or for other administrative offences.

64. Article 2.24 para. 6 of the Civil Code of the Republic of Lithuania.
65. The Republic of Lithuania Code of Administrative Offenses. Government Gazette 1985 No. 1-1.
66. Article 79 of the Code of Administrative Offences of the Republic of Lithuania.
67. Article 92 of the Code of Administrative Offences of the Republic of Lithuania.
68. Article 136 of the Code of Administrative Offences of the Republic of Lithuania.
69. Article 146 of the Code of Administrative Offences of the Republic of Lithuania.
70. Article 502 of the Code of Administrative Offences of the Republic of Lithuania.
71. Article 524 of the Code of Administrative Offences of the Republic of Lithuania.
72. Article 547 of the Code of Administrative Offences of the Republic of Lithuania.

III. Criminal Liability

84. Criminal liability as the *ultima ratio* measure may be applied against a journalist, like any other person, for the offenses specified in the criminal law which are considered dangerous and by which significant harm is inflicted on the interests of persons, society and those of the state.[73]

85. Under the Lithuanian law, both a journalist and a media may be brought to criminal liability for libel,[74] contempt for the memory of the deceased,[75] inciting discord[76] and in the presence of the elements of the criminal offence, for other offences defined in the Criminal Code of the Republic of Lithuania.

86. In the course of discussions between lawyers and journalists, the desire to strengthen freedom of expression and to avoid criminalization of insult when administrative and civil liability is applied/possible for this act has led to the decriminalization of insult as a criminal offence in Lithuania.[77]

§2. Is There a Special Liability Regime for Journalists? (Who Will Be Held Liable: Only the Journalist or Also the Publisher?)

87. Lithuanian laws do not provide for any specific liability regime applied to journalists. Depending on the remedy chosen, liability may be applied against the journalist personally, against the media/publisher or against them both.[78]

§3. Defamation and Libel

I. Defamation

88. A natural person's right to honour and dignity and a legal entity's right to professional reputation[79] may be defended by civil legal means. Under the provisions of Article 1.138 and Article 2.24 paragraph 1 of the Civil Code, persons who believe they have been defamed may request that the court:

(1) order the media and/or the journalist to refute untrue data which humiliate the person's honour and dignity;

73. Ruling of the Constitutional Court of the Republic of Lithuania of 10 Jun. 2003.
74. Article 154 of the Criminal Code of the Republic of Lithuania.
75. Article 313 of the Criminal Code of the Republic of Lithuania.
76. Article 170 of the Criminal Code of the Republic of Lithuania.
77. Until 25 Jun. 2015, Art. 155 of the Criminal Code of the Republic of Lithuania had laid down criminal liability for insult, however, by Law No XII-1888 of 25 Jun. 2015 (applicable from 10 Jul. 2015) (Register of Legal Acts, 2015, No. 2015-11179) the said criminal act was decriminalised.
78. Article 51 of the Law on Provision of Information to the Public of the Republic of Lithuania.
79. Article 2.24 para. 7 of the Civil Code of the Republic of Lithuania.

(2) request that the court adopts a decision by stating that the data disseminated by the media and/or the journalist are untrue and humiliate the natural person's honour and dignity and the legal entity's professional reputation;
(3) require compensation of pecuniary and non-pecuniary damage.

89. Where untrue data have been disseminated through the media (press, television, radio, etc.), the person about whom such data have been disseminated has the right to write a refutation and to demand that such refutation be printed out or otherwise made public free of charge by that media.[80]

90. The case law of the Lithuanian courts follows the jurisprudence of the European Court of Human Rights[81] which states that there must be an objective link between the claims of the dispute and the person bringing an action for defamation in order to benefit from the judicial protection of the damaged reputation; i.e., the relevant information must 'cast a shadow' on the person who is complaining about defamation.[82]

91. Besides, the case law of the Supreme Court of Lithuania upholds the position that the data disseminated about one entity may undermine the professional reputation of another entity when such entities are interrelated by certain links and such links are publicly known.[83] This includes the cases when the media or the journalist disseminates information which undermines the professional reputation of the legal entity and constitutes, as a derivative, a violation of the honour and dignity of the manager or shareholder of that legal entity.

II. Libel

92. In Lithuania, libel is a criminal offence (paragraph 84). The concept of libel as a criminal offence stems from Article 25 paragraph 4 of the Constitution. This mandatory provision has been transposed into Article 154 of the Criminal Code of the Republic of Lithuania under which libel includes the dissemination of false information about another person that could arouse contempt for this person or humiliate them, undermine trust in them. The said criminal offence is punished by a fine or restriction of liberty, arrest, or imprisonment for a term of one year.

93. When information disseminated about a person accuses them of the alleged commission of a serious or grave crime, or such information is disseminated in the media or in a publication, the criminal law lays down a more severe punishment by a fine or by arrest, or by imprisonment for a term of two years. The case law of the

80. Article 2.24 para. 2 of the Civil Code of the Republic of Lithuania.
81. Judgement of the European Court of Human Rights of 29 May 2001 in case *Thoma v. Luxembourg*, Petition No. 38432/97.
82. Judgement of the European Court of Human Rights of 31 Jul. 2007 in case *Dyuldin and Kislov v. Russia*, Case No. 25968/02.
83. Supreme Court of Lithuania, 25 Apr. 2014, Case No. 3K-3-234/2014.

Lithuanian courts contains individual cases when journalists were convicted for libel.[84] Though it should be noted, that through the twenty years the punishments in Lithuania for these crimes eased up. Imprisonment is not popularly used nowadays – only a few thousand euro fines.

§4. PRIVACY

94. The Constitutional Court has clarified that '[t]he legal concept of private life is linked with the state of an individual when the individual may expect privacy, or with legitimate expectations of private life.'[85]

95. Constitutional Court has stated[86] that one's privacy encompasses private, family and domestic life, the physical and psychological inviolability of individuals, their honour and reputation, the secrecy of personal facts, a prohibition on publicizing received or acquired confidential information, etc. If the private life of an individual is interfered with an arbitrary and unlawful manner, then, alongside, his honour and dignity are encroached upon. Important to notice, that it does not matter if the published information is true or not, a person whose right to privacy was violated has a strong ground to ask for damages.

96. A person's right to privacy and secrecy[87] is the constitutional norm[88] implemented in Article 2.23 of the Civil Code which lays down the following prohibitions:

(1) information on a person's private life may not be made public in the absence of the person's consent (paragraph 1);
(2) prohibition to collect information about the person's private life in violation of the laws (paragraph 3); and
(3) prohibition to disseminate the collected information about the person's private life.

84. Supreme Court of Lithuania, 18 Nov. 2020 Case no. BIK-548/2020; Supreme Court of Lithuania, 30 Mar. 2021 Case no. BIK-83/2021; Supreme Court of Lithuania, 27 Nov. 2001, Case No. 2K-1017.
85. Ruling of the Constitutional Court of the Republic of Lithuania of 8 May 2000.
86. Ruling of the Constitutional Court of the Republic of Lithuania of 21 Oct. 1999. Also, Ruling of the Constitutional Court of the Republic of Lithuania of 19 Sep. 2002. In addition to this, Ruling of the Constitutional Court of the Republic of Lithuania of 23 Oct. 2002.
87. The Constitutional Court of the Republic of Lithuania has clarified that '[t]he legal concept of private life is linked with the state of an individual when the individual may expect privacy, or with legitimate expectations of private life.' (Ruling of the Constitutional Court of the Republic of Lithuania of 8 May 2000).
88. Article 22 of the Constitution of the Republic of Lithuania.

97. On the other hand, the law admits that in certain cases, the collection and publication of information about a person's private life are justified based on a reasoned judgement of the court.[89] Information about the person's private life may be announced without the person's consent only in the following cases:[90]

(1) when information helps in the detection of violations of law or crimes;
(2) when information is presented during the open hearing of the case;
(3) when the information discloses the circumstances of the private life or the personal qualities of a public figure of public importance. However, such rules may not be applied literally by disregarding the common rules of the right to protection of private life.

98. As mentioned above, an exception to the restriction on the dissemination of collected information about a person's private life is applied to public persons.[91] The constitutional doctrine has clarified that 'the interest of the public to know more about these people than about others is constitutionally grounded.'[92] Public persons must tolerate the criticism directed at them (albeit not fully justified) which, in the case of a private individual, could be regarded as an affront to honour and dignity.[93]

99. Article 2.23 paragraph 3 of the Civil Code lays down that taking into consideration the person's official position and their status in the society, dissemination of the said information is in line with the lawful and well-grounded interest of the public to know such information. The Constitutional Court has underlined that when a person caries out actions of a public character and comprehends it or must comprehend it or is capable of understanding it, whether at home or other private premises, then such actions of a public character will not enjoy protection under Article 22 of the Constitution and the person may not expect privacy.[94]

100. However, it should be noted that the media may inform the public about the private life of such a person without the consent of the latter in as much as the

89. Article 2.23 para. 4 of the Civil Code of the Republic of Lithuania.
90. Article 14(3) of LPIP.
91. Public persons are understood as 'The state and municipal officials linked with the implementation of functions of state and municipal authority and administration are always of a public character' (Ruling of the Constitutional Court of the Republic of Lithuania of 8 May 2000). Also the 'persons participating in public and political activities' (Ruling of the Constitutional Court of the Republic of Lithuania of 23 Oct. 2002); also 'politicians, state and municipal officials, heads of public organisations. Other persons may also be considered public persons, if their activity is of importance to public affairs.' (Ruling of the Constitutional Court of the Republic of Lithuania of 23 Oct. 2002); state and municipal politicians, officials, heads of political parties and public organisations and other persons participating in public and political activities, i.e. participating in various public organisations, foundations and movements and well-known persons who influence public life – famous artists, sportsmen, journalists, representatives of other professions (Resolution of the Senate of the Supreme Court of Lithuania No. 1 'On the Republic of Lithuania'.
92. Ruling of the Constitutional Court of the Republic of Lithuania of 23 Oct. 2002.
93. Šindeikis, A. „Žodžio laisvė ir jos ribų kaita per du atkurtos nepriklausomybės dešimtmečius' ['Freedom of Speech and its Limits During Two Decades of Independence']. *Jurisprudencija* 20(3) (2013), 1040.
94. Ruling of the Constitutional Court of the Republic of Lithuania of 8 May 2000.

personal characteristics, behaviour and certain circumstances of the private life of the said person may be of importance to public affairs and due to this, the published information is of public importance.[95]

95. Ruling of the Constitutional Court of the Republic of Lithuania of 23 Oct. 2002.

Chapter 4. Right of Reply

101. In Lithuanian law, the 'right of reply' is granted to every natural person whose honour and dignity have been degraded by false, inaccurate or biased information published about them in the media. The same applies to any legal person whose professional reputation or other legitimate interests have been damaged by false, inaccurate or biased information.[96] The 'right of reply' includes:

(1) the right of reply by refuting the false information or correcting the published information, or
(2) the right to require that false information be refuted.[97]

102. Since the Resolution of the Council of Europe, Committee of Ministers No (74) 66 of 2 July 1974 'On the Right of Reply – Position of the Individual in Relation to the Press',[98] the right of reply is generally and *inter alia* recognized as one of the internationally established remedies for violated rights of the individual. This implies the right of an individual to reply to the media by refuting or correcting the disseminated information or by demanding the refutation of false information. In the Lithuanian legal framework, the right of reply is also understood as the mandatory pre-litigation dispute resolution procedure.[99] However, this pre-litigation dispute resolution procedure is mandatory only when (1) the information was announced by the media[100] and when (2) after a formal written application[101] by a person, the media refuses to announce a refutation, fails to do this on time or decides not to announce such refutation.

96. Article 15 of the LPIP.
97. *Ibid.*
98. https://rm.coe.int/16805048e1.
99. The case law of the Lithuanian courts upholds the position that '[a] pre-litigation out-of court dispute resolution procedure has two possible interpretations: as the activities of special out-of-court institutions which are regulated by law for the resolution of separate categories of disputes and as the necessity under the law to use the procedure of lodging claims, to try to settle with the opposite party and thus resolve a conflict.' (Order of the Vilnius County Court rendered on 15 Jan. 2019 in civil proceedings No e2A-48-781/2019).
100. The case law of the Lithuanian courts upholds the narrow approach and notes that the right of reply as laid down in Art. 2.24 paras 2 and 4 of the Civil Code of the Republic of Lithuania must be used by persons only when the data have been announced by the media. If the data have been announced through the media by another person and the media has communicated undistorted quotes of the person who has announced the data, the person about whom the data have been announced has the right to waive the right of reply and to address the court and request that the court order the person who has announced the data to refute the data adequately and to compensate the damage. (Order of the Supreme Court of Lithuania rendered on 2 Jul. 2020 in civil proceedings No. e3K-3-218-684/2020).
101. Although the Civil Code of the Republic of Lithuania does not lay down the form which must be used when addressing the media on the basis of Art. 2.24 of the Civil Code of the Republic of Lithuania, the case law recognises that, for example, e-mail messages are not considered as an official request to refute the announced false information (Vilnius County Court, 25 Sep. 2015, Case No. 2S-1783-340/2015).

103. The media has the right to refuse to print or announce refutation only in one case – when the content of the refutation is contrary to accepted principles of morality.[102] However, in the pre-litigation phase of the dispute, if the media refuses to refute the announced information without any good reason, the Lithuanian law, like in other countries, does not establish any liability for the failure to comply with such obligation.[103] In such a case, the person must defend their violated rights by judicial means and the media must assume the risk that in the event of a judicial decision unfavourable to the media, the media would be obliged not only to compensate for the damage[104] but, in the event of failure to comply with the judgement, would also pay a fine in the amount determined by the court for each day of non-compliance with the judgement.[105]

102. Article 2.24 para. 2 of the Civil Code of the Republic of Lithuania.
103. Liudvika Meškauskaitė, *Žiniasklaidos teisė, 2-as leidimas* [*Media Law*, 2nd ed.], Vilnius: Centre of Registers, 2018, 297.
104. The concept of 'damage' includes both pecuniary and non-pecuniary damage.
105. Article 2.24 para. 7 of the Civil Code of the Republic of Lithuania.

Chapter 5. Access to Public Information

§1. Public Documents and Meetings

104. A journalist as a public information professional is guaranteed the right to receive public information about other persons from state and/or municipal institutions following the procedure laid down by law. The expression of this constitutional right to receive, collect and disseminate information is established in Article 6 paragraph 1 of the LPIP. A journalist also has the right to obtain official documents (copies thereof) as well as any other information held by them about the person. Besides, journalists have the right under the law to obtain information from state authorities and municipal institutions and agencies faster.[106]

105. Given the fact that a journalist has the exclusive right to collect information about another person, there exists a clear state-wide regulation on what information is considered to be public and what procedure is applied for the receipt of public information about another person.

106. Under Article 2 paragraph 61 of the LPIP, public information means any information, except for the information which may not be disseminated to the public under the laws of the Republic of Lithuania.[107]

107. The procedure of receipt of public information about another person is described in detail in the Republic of Lithuania Law on the Right to Obtain Information from State and Municipal Institutions and Agencies.

108. Therefore, state and municipal institutions and bodies, other budgetary bodies which refuse to provide public information to the promoter of public information, must inform the promoter in writing of the reasons for refusing to provide information no later than the following working day.[108]

109. However, there are cases when state authorities make groundless attempts to restrict the media's access to public information. One such example was in December 2019 when the Ministry of National Defence of the Republic of Lithuania attempted to restrict the journalists' access to the draft Resolutions of the Government which were not yet adopted by marking them with the flag 'For Official Use Only'. Following the public outrage, the Ministry of National Defence of the Republic of Lithuania withdrew its draft amendment to the Law.[109]

---

106. Under Art. 6 para. 4 of the LPIP, information for the production whereof the accumulation of additional data is not required must be provided to the producers and/or disseminators of public information and journalists not later than within one working day, whereas information for the production whereof additional data has to be accumulated must be provided no later than within one week.
107. For example, a list of information which may not be disseminated in public is laid down in the Republic of Lithuania Law on State Secrets and Official.
108. Article 6 para. 5 of the LPIP.
109. For more information, see: https://rsf.org/en/lithuania.

110. The Supreme Administrative Court of Lithuania also issued an order in a case[110] of strong public interest when the Registry of the Government of the Republic of Lithuania refused to provide journalists with an audio recording of the meeting held by the Government. During the government meeting, the draft law on public information of the Republic of Lithuania was rejected, which proposed journalists to receive data free of charge from the state enterprise 'Registrų centras'. The Supreme Administrative Court of Lithuania, unlike the Court of First Instance,[111] ruled that the Government of the Republic of Lithuania, by refusing to provide journalists with an audio recording of the meeting held by the Government, violated the right of journalists to receive, collect and disseminate information.

111. Accredited Lithuanian or foreign journalists[112] also have the right to take part in the meetings and other events of the institution or organization they have been accredited with (e.g., the Seimas of the Republic of Lithuania, the Police Department).[113]

§2. Court Hearings and Documents

112. Journalists also have the right to obtain information by observing and recording in writing public judicial proceedings.[114] However, the right of journalists to take part in public hearings has been limited and the right of journalists to use technical means for gathering information during public hearings has been restricted in Lithuania since 1 July 2018. Currently, there is a prohibition[115] to film, take photographs, make audio or video recordings, broadcast the hearing, and use other technical means during a public hearing,[116] except for the announcement of a judicial decision.

113. The court may satisfy a journalist's written application and grant them permission to take part in the hearing at which a judicial decision will be announced. In such a case, a journalist is granted a possibility to record the judicial decision

110. Supreme Administrative Court of Lithuania, 23 Jul. 2020, Case No. eA-1639-520/2020.
111. The Vilnius Regional Court ruled that journalists had been provided with the minutes of the Government meeting, so the right of journalists to receive information and to disseminate correct information was guaranteed. Meanwhile, the Supreme Administrative Court of Lithuania noted that the content of the government meeting minutes submitted to journalists is highly laconic and uninformative, therefore does not guarantee the right of journalists to receive correct information.
112. Article 12 para. 3 of the LPIP lays down the right of the producer and/or disseminator of public information to accredit their journalists with state institutions, political parties, political organisations and associations as well as with other institutions by agreement between the parties.
113. Article 12 para. 2 of the LPIP.
114. Under Art. 9 para. 1 of the Code of Civil Procedure of the Republic of Lithuania, the hearings of matters are public in all courts, except the cases when in order to protect private or family life of a person and when a publicly heard matter may disclose a state, professional or commercial secret, or when a court takes steps to reconcile the parties.
115. Resolution of the Judicial Council No. 13P-46-(7.1.2) of 25 May 2018 'On the Approval of the Description of the Procedure of Use of Technical Means During the Announcement of a Judicial Decision'.
116. Article 38 para. 7 of the Republic of Lithuania Law on Courts.

with technical means, i.e., to film, take photographs or record the judge announcing the decision. However, it is prohibited to use any means to record other parties to the proceedings, including their representatives, and to record procedural documents and items.

114. As a rule, the material of all civil and enforcement proceedings the hearing whereof has been completed, except the proceedings the hearing whereof has been completed in-camera, is public. In light of the said principle, journalists have the right of access to the material and judicial decisions of completed cases and/or to make their copies (extracts), except the cases when the material of the case or any part thereof has been announced in public.[117]

115. An order of the court whereby a journalist's application to have access to the case material has been dismissed may be appealed against to the court of appellate instance by lodging a separate appeal.

117. Order of the Minister of Justice of the Republic of Lithuania No. 1R-308 of 7 December 2012 'On the Approval of the Rules of Access to the Material of the Cases the Hearing Whereof has been completed in Courts'.

Chapter 6. Councils of Press and Broadcasting

§1. Ethics Commission of Journalists and Publishers

116. The Commission as a collegial member, as well as a regulatory institution, of the association of the Provision of Information to the Public,[118] examines violations of professional ethics done by producers or disseminators of public information when providing information to the public. The Commission also examines persons' complaints with regard to activities of producers and disseminators of public information who have allegedly infringed the provisions of the Code of Ethics of Lithuanian Journalists and Publishers. It also examines disputes between producers and disseminators of public information regarding violations of the Ethics Code.[119]

117. The Commission of Publishers consists of one member delegated from each of the following 15 organizations uniting public information producers, disseminators and journalists: Lithuanian Center for Human Rights, Lithuanian Psychiatric Association, Lithuanian Catholic Church Bishops' Conference, Lithuanian Periodical Publishers Association, Lithuanian Radio and Television Association, Lithuanian Cable Television Association, Lithuanian Television Association, Lithuanian Journalists' Association, Lithuanian Journalism Center, LRT, the Association of Publishers of Magazines, the Association of Publishers of Regional Press, the National Association of Publishers of District and Urban Newspapers, the Association of Communication and Advertising Agencies (hereinafter 'the Meeting'). The members of the Commission shall be appointed for three years. Organizations of journalists and publishers who delegate their representatives to the Commission shall hold meetings attended by at least three delegates from each of these organizations at least once a calendar year. The meeting approves the rules of procedure of the Commission.[120]

118. Decisions of the Commission, regarding infringements of professional ethics or other violations must be immediately announced in that media in which the Commission has established the said violations, as well as in accordance with the procedure for publishing refutation as laid down in Article 44 of LPIP. If a producer and/or disseminator of public information fails to announce within two weeks a decision of the Commission regarding the infringement of professional ethics or other violations in its medium, the said decision of the Commission regarding the infringement of professional ethics or other violations is announced through the first channel of the Lithuanian national radio and the costs of such announcement are covered by the producer and/or disseminator of public information in respect of whom the said decision has been taken. This decision is also announced on the website of the Association.[121]

118. Article 46(1) of the LPIP.
119. Article 46(4) of the LPIP.
120. Article 46(2) of the LPIP.
121. Article 46(7) of the LPIP.

119. Producers or disseminators of public information who do not accept the decisions of the Commission may apply to Vilnius Regional Administrative Court.[122] However, they still must announce the said decisions in accordance with the procedure (paragraph 118).

§2. Radio and Television Commission of Lithuania

120. The Radio and Television Commission of Lithuania (LRTK) investigates user complaints concerning the activities of broadcasters of radio and/or television programmes and providers of on-demand audiovisual media services. LRTK is an expert for the Seimas and government, regarding questions about radio and television broadcasting and retransmission issues.[123]

121. The LRTK consists of 13 members of which one member is appointed by the President of the Republic, three members are appointed by the Seimas on the recommendation of the Committee on Culture, and then one member each is appointed by: Lithuanian Artists' Union, Lithuanian Cinematographers' Union, Lithuanian Composers' Union, Lithuanian Writers' Union, Lithuanian Theater Union, Lithuanian Journalists' Association, Lithuanian Catholic Church Bishops' Conference, Lithuanian Periodical Publishers' Association.

122. Only a citizen of the Republic of Lithuania of impeccable reputation may be appointed a member of the Commission. The members of the Commission may serve for a maximum of two terms of office of the public authority which appointed them or for a maximum of twice the term of office of the governing bodies of the appointing authority.[124] No other qualifications are required to apply for this position that is established by law.

122. Article 46(8) of the LPIP.
123. Article 47 of the LPIP.
124. Article 47(4) of the LPIP.

Part III. Regulation of Audiovisual Media (Broadcasting)

Chapter 1. Public Service Broadcasting

§1. HISTORY

123. The Ruling of the Constitutional Court of 21 December 2006[125] analyses the history of the establishment of the Lithuanian national public broadcasting in detail:

> In Lithuania, public radio broadcasts began on 13 June 1926. The Law on Radio Communications (wording of 30 March 1933 with subsequent amendments) regulated the relations of the establishment of radio transition and reception stations, import and registration of radio sets and distribution of fees for them. Under this law, every citizen of Lithuania, after he has registered his radio set and paid the subscription fee, could use radio reception sets, while after the reception of a permit from the Minister of Communications, he could also use radio transmission sets.
>
> On 22 March 1927, Seimas adopted the Law on Radio Stations' Tariffs whereby it established fees for radio stations installed in public places (restaurants, clubs), establishments, private apartments and similar places. The Radio Tariff was abolished on 16 January 1935 after the President of the Republic promulgated the Law on Post, Telegraph, Telephone and Radio Tariffs (it was applied even for some time after the Soviet Union occupied Lithuania in 1940).
>
> Besides, on 26 March 1929, the President of the Republic promulgated the Law on the State Radiophone. Art 1 of this law prescribed that the State Radiophone shall be designed for 'dissemination of scientific, art, information and other cultural news', while Art 9 provided that 'the receipts of the State Radiophone shall be composed, inter alia, from the subscription and registration fees of radio sets, which is established by law, receipts from concerts and radio adverts, as well as the sums allocated from the budget'.
>
> ... . After the Soviet Union occupied Lithuania, on the first day of the occupation, on 15 June 1940, the Soviet troops captured the State Radiophone as well.

125. Ruling of the Constitutional Court of the Republic of Lithuania of 21 December 2006 'On status, management and rights of the national broadcaster'.

By the Resolution (No. 265) 'On the Reorganisation of the State Radiophone of the Lithuanian Soviet Socialist Republic (hereinafter – Lithuanian SSR)' of 26 October 1940 of the then Soviet of People's Commissars of the Lithuanian SSR, the then State Radiophone was reorganized into the Radiofication and Radiophony Committee under the Soviet People's Commissars of the Lithuanian SSR.

... . During World War II, when Lithuania was occupied by Germany, the Radiophone of Kaunas (August 1941) and later the Vilnius Radio were connected to the radio network of Germany.

... . At the end of World War II (summer of 1944), when the Soviet troops occupied Lithuania again and consolidated the occupation power in its territory, the Lithuanian radio was subjected to totalitarian governance and became a tool of Soviet propaganda.

... . In Lithuania, television appeared in the sixth decade of the 20th century, i.e., much later than in most European states.

... . The Lithuanian Television was established by order No. 71 of 25 February 1957 issued by the Minister of Culture of the then Lithuanian SSR whereby the Vilnius television studio was established; pursuant to order No. 194 of 30 April 1957 issued by the Minister of Culture of the Lithuanian SSR the broadcast of state television programmes began.

... . The broadcasts of the Lithuanian radio as well as of television were strictly censored during the Soviet occupation. The Lithuanian television, as well as radio, was a state establishment and from the start, it used to be (until television appeared and for some time later) under the jurisdiction of the Ministry of Culture, while as of June 1957 it was under the jurisdiction of the Radio and Television Committee under the Soviet of Ministers of the Lithuanian SSR.

... . On 11 March 1990, when the independent State of Lithuania was restored, the first preconditions were created for the Lithuanian Radio and Television to become a public broadcaster, i.e., to discharge the function that the State Radiophone used to discharge in many respects until the Soviet and German occupations.

... . On 22 March 1990, the Supreme Council of the Republic of Lithuania adopted the Republic of Lithuania's Law 'On the Reorganisation of the State Television and Radio Committee of the Republic of Lithuania' by Item 1 whereof the State Television and Radio Committee was abolished and the Lithuanian Radio and Television was established.

On the same day, on 22 March 1990, the Supreme Council adopted the Resolution (No. I-60) 'On the Board of the Lithuanian Radio and Television' in which it was prescribed that the Supreme Council shall form the Board of the Lithuanian Radio and Television from 15 representatives of society and employees of the Lithuanian Radio and Television.

The Supreme Council adopted the Resolution (No. I-208) 'On Approving the Statute of the Lithuanian Radio and Television' on 10 May 1990, whereby the Statute of the Lithuanian Radio and Television was approved. The Statute of the Lithuanian Radio and Television, which was approved by the said resolution, prescribed, inter alia, that the Lithuanian National Radio and Television (hereinafter 'the LRT') shall manage the equipment of the preparation of programmes and shall use transmission equipment by the priority right.

.... By these first Supreme Council acts designed for regulation of the relations linked with the LRT, preconditions were created to seek to attain that the LRT become independent from state institutions (their officials), that neither state institutions (their officials), nor other persons interfere with the activities of the LRT. Such independence was a necessary condition for LRT to become a public broadcaster.

On 13 January 1991, the troops of the Soviet Union captured the Lithuanian Radio and Television (in Vilnius) by force and discontinued the transmission. However, the transmission of Lithuanian television broadcasts was soon renewed by creating alternative networks of transmission from other stations (from Kaunas, as well as from a studio in the Supreme Council of the Republic of Lithuania). On 22 August 1991, the occupation troops were forced to leave the captured buildings of the Lithuanian Radio and Television.

§2. The Concept and Mission of Public Service Broadcasting

124. Lithuania has a dual broadcasting system: public service broadcasting and private broadcasting (paragraphs 29–33).

125. Public service broadcasting is guaranteed by the LRT. It is a public non-profit institution that, according to the right of ownership, belongs to the State.

126. The LNRT[126] sets out the procedure of the founding, administration, activity, reorganization and liquidation of the LRT, as well as defines its rights, obligations and liability.

127. The Constitutional Court has held that the implementation of the public interest, as an interest of society, which is recognized by the state and is protected by law, is one of the most important conditions of the existence and evolution of society itself'.[127] According to the Constitutional Court, the same can be said about the interest of society to be informed. The free and universal exchange of information and its unrestricted dissemination are a particularly important factor in democratic processes. This factor ensures not only the formation of individual opinion and subjective convictions but also that of group views, including political, as well as that of the whole Nation's will.[128]

128. Under constitutional obligation, public broadcasting not only should not hinder the free flow of information and ideas, and to take all necessary measures so that other persons would not hinder it, but also to resort to measures (positive activity) itself (through its institutions). That is how the public would be informed about

126. Official Gazette 2020-05-22, No. 10874.
127. Rulings of the Constitutional Court of 6 May 1997, 13 May 2005, and 21 Sep. 2006.
128. Ruling of the Constitutional Court of 13 Feb. 1997.

the most important processes taking place in society and the state, that citizens (and other residents) would receive information as precisely as possible about the things that they have to know. People could also participate in the adoption of decisions of state importance, participate in the adoption of other decisions related with managing public affairs, as well as decision-related with the implementation of their rights and freedoms.

129. Otherwise, preconditions would be created not only to violate the rights of the person (including the right of citizens consolidated in Paragraph 1 of Article 33 of the Constitution to participate in the governance of their state both directly and through their democratically elected representatives and the right of citizens consolidated in Paragraph 2 of the same article to criticize the work of state institutions or their officials and to appeal against their decisions), but also other values which are entrenched in and defended and protected by the Constitution.[129]

130. It needs to be specially emphasized that important functions fall upon the public broadcaster, who carries out its mission, in contributing to the implementation of the sovereignty of the Nation and principles of democracy. It also ensures the security of society and the state, public order, welfare of the citizens and their rights and freedoms. An important role falls upon the public broadcaster when the state discharges its constitutional obligation to support culture and science, to take care of the protection of Lithuanian historical, artistic and cultural monuments and other culturally valuable objects.[130]

131. In the light of such understanding of the Constitution, Article 3 of the LNRT defines the mission of the public service broadcasting in the following manner:

> 'The National Radio and Television of Lithuania must collect and publish information concerning Lithuania and the world, acquaint the public with the variety of European and world culture, fundamentals of the current civilization, reinforce the independence and democracy of the Republic of Lithuania, create, nurture and protect the values of national culture, foster tolerance, and humanism, the culture of cooperation, intellection and language, strengthen public morality and civic awareness, develop country's ecological culture. The programmes shall be of good quality in terms of content, form and language. In preparing and broadcasting its coverage the National Radio and Television of Lithuania must be guided by the principles of objectivity, democracy and impartiality, ensure freedom of speech and creativity, must reflect in its broadcasts diverse opinions and convictions/beliefs, with individuals of various certitudes having the right to take part and voice their views in them. Human dignity and human rights must be respected in the broadcasts, and the principles of morality and ethics must not be violated.'

129. Ruling of the Constitutional Court of 21 December 2006.
130. Ruling of the Constitutional Court of 21 December 2006.

132. Article 4 of the LNRT sets out requirements for the programmes of the LRT aimed at fulfilling its mission. The article regulates that a variety of topics and genres must be ensured in the programmes of the LRT. The broadcasts must be oriented towards the various strata of society and people of different ages, various nationalities, and convictions. One-sided political views should not be allowed to predominate in the programmes. The programmes of the LRT shall reflect the plurality of topics and genres, the information presented in information broadcasts and commentaries of the National Radio and Television of Lithuania must be substantiated and reflect various political views, while opinions and factual news must be authorized, verified and comprehensive.[131] According to Article 4(2) LNRT, priority shall be accorded to national culture as well as informative programmes, programmes of world culture, journalistic, analytical, cognitive, educational, art and sports programmes. Mass culture shall be reflected in review, cognitive and analytical broadcasts. With respect to the protection of the Lithuanian language, audiovisual works of art in a foreign language shall be translated into Lithuanian language or subtitled.[132] The Council of the LRT shall establish a proportion of audiovisual works of art in a foreign language to be translated into Lithuanian language or subtitled.

133. Article 3(3) of the LNRT sets out that the broadcasting coverage of the LRT shall be the entire territory of the Republic of Lithuania. During strikes by the employees of the LRT, the radio and television must ensure for its listeners and viewers, the minimum of information, which shall be stipulated by the Council of the National Radio and Television of Lithuania.[133] In the event of natural disasters, epidemics, an extraordinary or war situation, the LRT must broadcast the official statements of the President, Seimas, Government, Constitutional Court and Office of the Prosecutor General.[134] The norms are the guarantees of the constitutional rights of every person set out in Article 25(1)–25(3) of the Constitution:

(1) The human being shall have the right to have his convictions and freely express them.
(2) The human being must not be hindered from seeking, receiving and spreading information and ideas.
(3) Freedom to express beliefs, to receive and spread information may not be limited otherwise than by law if this is necessary to protect the health, honour and dignity, private life, and morals of a human being, or to defend the constitutional order.

134. The National Radio and Television of Lithuania has the right to frequencies for two television (LRT TELEVIZIJA, LRT PLIUS) and three radio channels

131. Article 4(1) of the LNRT.
132. Article 4(4) of the LNRT.
133. Article 8(1) of the LNRT.
134. Article 8(2) of the LNRT.

(LRT RADIJAS, LRT KLASIKA, LRT OPUS). It also broadcasts outside Lithuania's territory – channel for Lithuanians around the world LRT LITUANICA and the news portal LRT.lt.

135. To inform society and reflect on various political views, the LRT has the right of free recording and transmission of the Seimas and Government meeting proceedings, and formal acts of the state and using the recordings according to its own discretion.[135] It also allocates the broadcasting time to the President of the Republic of Lithuania to speak on issues of domestic and foreign policy in the procedure set out in the Law on the President of the Republic of Lithuania, also allocate the broadcasting time as soon as possible to official announcements of Seimas, the Government or opposition (Article 5(7)).

136. To reach the various groups of society and people of different ages, various nationalities and convictions, Article 5(8) of the Law sets out that the LRT shall have the duty to provide time for Lithuania's traditional and state-recognized religious communities to broadcast religious services under the conditions and procedure stipulated in bilateral agreements. Article 5(9) of the Law establishes the duty of the national broadcaster to prepare broadcasts designed for national minorities to disseminate their culture. Article 5(10) of the Law establishes the duty of the LRT to prepare broadcasts or programmes designed for persons with hearing and visual disabilities.

137. The freedom of broadcasting – public as well as private – is protected at the constitutional level from the influencing and using broadcasting by the State for its purposes. In this regard, Article 44 of the Constitution sets out that censorship of mass information shall be prohibited. The State, political parties, political and public organizations, and other institutions or persons may not monopolize the mass media.

138. According to LPIP, radio and/or television programmes broadcasting activities pursued by the LRT shall not be licenced. In order to ensure the broadcasting of the LRT radio and/or television programmes, the LRTK of Lithuania shall, without tender in order of priority and in accordance with the provisions and conditions set out in this law, issue authorizations granting the rights equivalent to those granted by the licences. In its' ruling of 20 April 1995, the Constitutional Court[136] gave the regulation stating that the LRT shall have the priority right to use of the equipment of transmission, as well as of the network of radio relay lines, does not contradict the Constitution.

139. In its' ruling of 21 December 2006, the Constitutional Court held that 'the activity of the public broadcaster cannot be commercialized, its programmes and broadcasts should not be oriented to attracting the biggest possible audience, nor to

135. Article 5(2) of the LNRT.
136. Ruling of the Constitutional Court of 20 Apr. 1995 'On the Statute of the Radio and Television of Lithuania'.

commercial success. The public broadcaster must not adapt to the situation in the audience or the market, not flatter consumerist tastes, but inform and educate the society, implant such civil and cultural attitudes in the public, which are dictated to the public broadcaster by its constitutional mission. If one deviated from this requirement, not only the constitutional mission of the public broadcaster would be harmed, but also the *raison d'être* of the public broadcaster would be negated'.

140. Therefore, its purpose cannot be merely striving for a bigger audience of listeners or viewers, nor satisfaction of consumerist needs. Quite to the contrary, the public broadcaster, without representing any interest group, must render public radio and television services to the entire society, and not only to its founder, i.e. the state. The programmes and broadcasts of the public broadcaster must be prepared and disseminated not because of their economic profit, but because the corresponding information is necessary for the citizens (and other residents) so that the citizens might participate in the adoption of decisions of state importance, other decisions related with the management of public affairs, as well as decisions related with the implementation of their rights and freedoms.

§3. The Organization of Public Service Broadcasting

141. As stated above, the public service broadcasting is offered by the National Radio and Television of Lithuania that is a public non-profit institution according to the right of ownership belonging to the State. Article 5(1) of the LNRT indicates that there may not be any other owners of the National Radio and Television of Lithuania.

142. Though the LRT is established by the State, it is an independent legal body. The Constitutional Court has stressed that 'the law must establish such model of governance of the public broadcaster, which would ensure that one will not deviate from the constitutional mission of the public broadcaster, also that independence of the public broadcaster will not be denied'.[137] This is guaranteed through the current management system – the Council and the Director.

I. Council

143. The Constitutional Court has held that 'the public broadcaster established by the state may reasonably be regarded as a public broadcaster only when the institution that has the powers to decide the most important issues of the activity of the public broadcaster is composed not of state officials or servants, but from persons who could be reasonably called representatives of the entire society, but not of some interest groups (as well as professional and institutionalized groups, inter alia, those linked with mass media, with radio and television in particular, as well as groups uniting the persons whose creative work or production could be promoted by the

137. Ruling of the Constitutional Court of 21 December 2006.

public broadcaster). They must express namely the interests of the entire society. These persons must represent the widest possible social spectrum'.[138]

144. By the LNRT, the functions of the general meeting of the National Radio and Television of Lithuania are assigned to the Council of the National Radio and Television of Lithuania (Article 5(1)) (hereinafter 'the Council') which is the highest-ranking organ representing the interests of the general public (Article 9(2)). In its ruling on 21 April 1998, the Constitutional Court[139] explained that the LRT Council is not a part of the authorities of the state, thus the legal status of a Council member is not equivalent to that of a state official or state officer.

145. According to the LNRT, the term of office for the members of the Council is 6 years, there is a possibility to repeat this term once. There are 12 members of the Council. It is to be composed of the representatives of society in general, science and culture. The members of the Council are assigned in the following procedure: 4 members are assigned by the President of the Republic of Lithuania, 4 members (2 of them shall be of opposition) – by Seimas, 4 members – by four institutions: Research Council of Lithuania, Educational Council of Lithuania, Association of Lithuanian Artists and Lithuanian Bishops Conference.[140] Members of the Seimas, Government, the LRTK of Lithuania, public official of political (personal) confidence[141] and also persons who are in labour relationships with radio and television stations, including the National Radio and Television of Lithuania, and also the owners and co-owners of radio and television stations, may not be members of the Council.

146. In comparison to members of the Ethics Commission, where the only requirement is impeccable reputation, only citizens of the Republic of Lithuania of impeccable reputation must be appointed to the Council, but they must also have a higher university education, a master's degree or equivalent higher education qualification and 5 years of work experience (criteria, when a person cannot have an impeccable reputation are defined in the Law on Civil Service of the Republic of Lithuania).[142]

147. The composition procedure of the Council is organized by the Seimas Committee of Culture. It also summons the first meeting of the Council where the chairman of the Council shall be elected by the majority of Council members' votes to serve a three-year term. The deputy of the chairman is elected by the majority of votes at the same time.

---

138. *Ibid.*
139. Ruling of the Constitutional Court of 21 Apr. 1998 'On the Lithuanian National Radio and Television and on dismissing the Prosecutor General from Office'.
140. Article 10(2) of the LNRT.
141. Public official of political (personal) confidence means a civil servant recruited for a term of office of the appointing state politician or the appointing collegiate state institution or for a term specified in other laws.
142. Article 10(3) of the LNRT.

148. Due to the impartiality of the public broadcaster from the State, the member of the Council may not be recalled from the office during their term, except when:

- they step down;
- they finish the term of office;
- they die;
- they fail to participate in the Council's work for more than four months without a reasonable excuse;
- they lose the impeccable reputation, or it becomes clear that they did not have the qualifications (paragraph 146) to apply for the position in the first place;
- they lose the citizenship of the Republic of Lithuania;
- the Chief Commission for Official Ethics adopts a decision regarding a gross violation of the provisions of the Law on the Coordination of Public and Private Interests of the Council of Lithuania.

149. A member shall serve in the Council no longer than two consecutive terms of office.

150. The Council is responsible for the strategy of the programmes, as well as for the strategy of the LRT itself. The human resources issue falls under the competence of the Council, as well. The Council is responsible for organizing the election procedure of the Director of the LRT and for appointing them. The Council also forms permanent Administrative commissions which are responsible for the financial and economic issues of the public broadcaster.[143]

151. The activity of the Council is public. It is authorized to organize closed-door hearings upon the procedure established in the regulation of the activity of the Council. All decisions of the Council are made public.

152. The chairmen of the Council once a year account for the activity of the Council before Seimas.

153. Lithuanian authors argue that the formation procedure of the Council and the length of term (6 years) do not fully meet the principle of impartiality, thus the term shall be shortened, the number of representatives from state institutions shall be reduced or shall be totally replaced by the representatives of the academic and legal society.[144]

---

143. Article 11(1) of the LNRT.
144. L Meškauskaitė, *Žiniasklaidos teisė, 2-as leidimas* [*Media Law*, 2nd ed.], Vilnius: Vilniaus universiteto Teisės fakultetas, 2018, 195, 199.

II. Functions, Rights and Accountability of the General Director of LRT

154. Director is the general manager and representative of the LRT domestically, abroad and in international organizations. Director prepares the annual report of activities of the LRT and submits it to the Council for approval.

155. The General Director also establishes and approves the structure of the LRT; concludes agreements; issues orders and controls their implementation; implements the goals and objectives of the LRT and the strategy set by the Council; organizes the implementation of Council resolutions; at the request of the Council; informs the Council about the implementation of the functions of the LRT provided for by law and the resolutions of the Council; resolves other issues assigned to the competence of the General Director in the Articles of Association of the LRT. The General Director also receives the resolutions of the Council and gets acquainted with them, gets acquainted with the reports of the LRT Ethics Controller, the head of the LRT Internal Audit Service, other information necessary for the performance of their functions and may participate in Council and committee meetings without the right to vote. The General Director of the LRT prepares and submits the annual report on the activities of the LRT to the Council for approval.

156. The Director is appointed for a 5-year term through a public tender procedure by a simple majority of the votes of the Council. A member of the Council shall not be appointed the director of the LRT. If the required number of votes is not obtained, a new competition shall be held. Only a citizen of the Republic of Lithuania of impeccable reputation, who has obtained a higher university or equivalent education degree, has a master's degree or an equivalent higher education qualification and 5 years of managerial work experience, may be appointed the General Director. The criteria for a person to be considered of good repute are defined in the Civil Service Act.

157. In addition to that, only a citizen of the Republic of Lithuania with an impeccable reputation, a university degree or equivalent, a master's degree or equivalent higher education qualification and 5 years of managerial experience may be appointed Deputy General Director of the LRT. The criteria for a person to be considered of good repute are defined in the Civil Service Act. The Deputy Directors-General shall be appointed for the term of office of the General Director

158. Should the individual who has been approved as a General Director, be a member of a political party or a political organization, he (she) shall suspend the membership in that organization during the term of service. In addition, members of the Seimas, the Government, the Lithuanian Radio and Television Commission, and civil servants of political (personal) confidence may not be elected General Director. Persons involved in the employment relationship with radio and television broadcasters, as well as radio and/or television broadcasters, controllers of the information media (legal entities) and their participants, members of the governing bodies, members of the Supervisory Board shall resign immediately after their appointment as General Director. Auditors or employees of audit companies who are and/or have been involved in the audit of the LRT, from which 2 years have not elapsed, may not be elected as the General Director. The General Director may not work for business, commerce or other institutions, companies or organizations, and may not receive any remuneration other than remuneration determined by his/her current position and remuneration for scientific and pedagogical work and royalties for creative activities.[145]

159. General Director may be dismissed from office by two-thirds of the votes of the Council due to mistrust. Director may resign from office prior to the expiration of the term. In case of resignation of the Council, the General Director, appointed by it, shall be dismissed from office.[146]

III. LRT etikos kontrolierius[147]

160. In accordance with the principles of legality, impartiality, justice, independence, and publicity, the LRT Ethics Ombudsperson monitors LRT journalists' compliance with the Code of Ethics for Public Information, the Resolution of the Parliamentary Assembly of the Council of Europe on journalism ethics and the basic rules and principles of professional ethics. The Ethics Ombudsperson also examines and prepares responses to complaints of individuals regarding violations of the rules of journalistic ethics in accordance with its competence.

161. The LRT Ethics Ombudsperson shall be appointed and dismissed by the Council through public competition for a term of 5 years. The LRT Ethics Officer may hold office for a maximum of two consecutive terms. Only a citizen of the Republic of Lithuania of impeccable reputation with a master's degree in humanities or social sciences or an equivalent higher education qualification and at least 5 years of work experience in the specialty may be appointed LRT Ethics Ombudsperson. The criteria for a person to be considered of good repute are defined in the Civil Service Act.

162. If a person appointed as the LRT Ethics Ombudsperson is a member of a political party or political organization, he or she shall suspend his or her membership in this organization for the period of being the LRT Ethics Ombudsperson. Members of the Seimas, the Government, the Lithuanian Radio and Television Commission, the Inspector of Ethics of Journalists, members of the political (personal) trust, members of municipal councils, the General Director of the LRT, their deputy or another employee of the LRT, as well as persons related to the employment relations with radio and/or television broadcasters, as well as radio and/or television broadcasters, information society media (legal entities) managers and/or their participants, members of management bodies, members of the Supervisory Board,

---

145. Article 13(4) of the LNRT.
146. Article 13(5) of the LNRT.
147. Article 15 of the LNRT.

auditors or employees of audit firms, participating in and/or have participated in the audit of the LRT, from which 2 years have not elapsed.

163. The Ethics Ombudsperson of the LRT may be removed from office before the end of his/her term of office due to distrust expressed by the Council, if at least 2/3 of all members of the Council vote in favour.

164. The LRT Ethics Officer may not be removed from office before the expiry of his or her term of office.[148]

§4. The Financing of Public Service Broadcasting

165. Since 1996 the LPIP provided that the national broadcaster shall be financed through the state resources and from the State levy, as well as from the income received for the sale of broadcasts, publishing and other commercial activity. With the increase of the LRT financing from the State levy, the LRT financing from the State Budget shall be reduced accordingly. The same article set out that the State levy shall be introduced by an act of Seimas (Article 29). However, such an act was never adopted. Thus, the State budget is the main resource financing of the LRT.

166. Since 1 January 2001, the financing of the LRT is regulated by the Law on the LRT (version of 29 June 2000). The first version of this law in Article 15 set out identical norms as the above-mentioned norms of the LPIP. However, Article 6(4) of the Law on the LRT additionally set out that with the increase of the LRT income obtained from the State levy, advertising time shall be gradually and proportionately reduced from 15% of a day's broadcast time to 10%. The norms were due to come into force as of the 1 January 2001. However, Seimas did not adopt legislation for the introduction of the said broadcasting levy directly paid by the public, thus the effective date was postponed several times until 1 January 2006. Meanwhile, on 22 December 2005, Seimas adopted the new version of the Law on the LRT which came into force on 31 December 2005. It did not set out the broadcasting levy as the funding source for the public broadcaster.

167. In its ruling of 21 December 2006, the Constitutional Court held that 'the nature and constitutional mission of the public broadcaster … imply not only the state obligation to establish the public broadcaster, but also a duty to ensure the activity of the public broadcaster, *inter alia*, a duty to assign proper financing to the public broadcaster so that it could carry out the said mission and render corresponding public broadcasting services.' In the same ruling, the Constitutional Court

148. Except in cases where: he/she loses the citizenship of the Republic of Lithuania; he/she does not meet the requirements of having an impecable reputation, he/she does not meet the requirements of para. 4, mentioned above; he/she resigns; he/she shall be relieved from his/hers duties at the end of his/hers term of office; he/she dies.

declared that the norms allowing broadcasting of commercial advertising in programmes of the LRT were not in conflict with the Constitution, since in 2015 commercial advertising was banned by the amendments of the Law on the LRT.[149] In fact, commercial advertising[150] generated a considerable portion of the LRT revenue till the amendments. Thus, more sound financing from the State budget was granted by the Law. Now the funding of the public broadcaster is mainly through the State budget resources. The annual finances of the LRT through the State budget amount to 1.5% of the annual individual income tax and 1.3% of the annual excise income. The LRT may also gain income from the sale of programmes, publishing, donations, as well as commercial and economic activity (Article 15(1) and 15(5) of the Law on the LRT).

168. In the ruling of 21 December 2006, the Constitutional Court declared that Article 15(2) of the LNRT version of 29 June 2000) set out that 'the LRT shall engage in commercial … activity independently' did not contradict the Constitution. However, the Constitutional Court has analysed this norm only in the context of the right of the LRT to broadcast commercial advertising. As stated above, commercial advertising by the LRT was abolished on 1 January 2015. However, the current version of the Law still sets out that 'the LRT shall engage in commercial, economic and publishing activity independently under the procedure set out by this law'. The Law does not set out any specific procedure for implementing commercial, economic and publishing activity by the LRT, thus the content of its right to engage in commercial activity remains somewhat unclear.

169. As in the previous version of the Law, the current version sets out that the assets of the LRT are the State assets and may not be privatized. The public broadcaster manages the assets, uses, and disposes of them based on the trust agreement.

170. In addition to the management of these state-owned assets, LRT also manages, uses and disposes of the assets owned by it.[151]

149. In the same ruling the Constitutional Court also stated that 'The legislature may even prohibit broadcasting advertising on the national radio and television at all (although it is a rare case in the world), but only if the resources and financial possibilities of society can afford it and if it does not impair the constitutional mission of the national public broadcaster. In addition, in such a special situation the legislature must ensure the proper financing of the LRT as the national public broadcaster in other ways, for example, by means of the so-called subscription fee (levy), especially if the complete ban on advertising broadcasting might prevent this broadcaster from carrying out its constitutional mission.'
150. With certain limitations, e.g., maximum advertising time could have amounted to 15% of a day's broadcast time; advertising during the broadcast of films less than forty-five minutes length was limited, advertising was banned on days of mourning announced by the State, during broadcasts of events of State significance, during broadcasts intended for children and during informative and educative broadcasts. Teleshopping ads were also prohibited.
151. state-invested assets; income received from LRT commercial and economic activities; funds and other assets received as a support under the Law on Charity and support of the Republic of Lithuania; other monetary funds, except for the state budget funds; assets acquired from the state budget and the funds provided for in items 2, 3 and 4 of this Part, except for real estate acquired with the support of the European Union, state budget and state funds; donated property; inherited property;

171. The assets of the LRT referred to in Paragraph 2 of this Article shall be managed, used and disposed of per the procedure established by the Council and by concluding only such civil transactions that do not contradict the founding documents and objectives of the LRT. LRT buildings and land may not be sold, transferred or mortgaged.

172. Fixed assets, except for LRT buildings and land, the residual value of each object of which is not less than EUR 50,000, may be sold, transferred or written off by LRT only with the permission of the Government. Fixed assets, except for LRT buildings and land, the residual value of each object of which is less than EUR 50,000, may be sold, transferred or written off by LRT with the permission of the Council.[152]

173. The LRT may dispose of the completely depreciated long-term and short-term assets by the decision of the Director (Article 18(6) of the LNRT).

174. The LRT is not subject to bankruptcy rules. It shall be liquidated or reorganized only by an act of Seimas (Articles 19(4) and 20 of the LNRT).

property rights arising from the results of intellectual activity; income, assets or other benefits derived from the management, use and disposal of the funds or other assets referred to above.

152. Article 18 of the LNRT.

Chapter 2. Private Broadcasting

§1. Fair Competition in the Field of Broadcasting

175. During the first years of restored independent Lithuania, legal acts of the Government and the Supreme Council of Lithuania[153] created preconditions for private broadcasters to compete with the LRT for the audience of listeners and viewers. By the Government Resolution No. 62 'On Renting Radio and Television Networks' of 31 January 1992 the Ministry of Communications and Informatics was granted the right to rent (upon assent by the Government or the Supreme Council of Lithuania) state radio and television transmitters, wire radiofication and cable television networks, including those which had been rented to the LRT. On 6 February 1992, the Presidium of the Supreme Council of Lithuania by its Resolution No. I-2293 'On the Independent System of Mass Information' approved the decision of the LRT to establish an independent non-state television by using the third television channel.

176. Private Limited Liability Company 'Tele-3' at the end of 1992 was granted the licence to use the third television channel. The first private broadcast aired on 11 April 1993. Within several years it was joined by several other private broadcasters.

177. The Constitutional Court has held that 'The interest of society to be informed which is guaranteed and protected by the Constitution, as well as the constitutional freedom of information, can be ensured only when various mass media function freely (it does not mean that without restrictions) in the state. A mature and developed system of mass media is a necessary condition for ensuring the public interest, i.e. the interest of society, to be informed. The freedom of mass media, as well as the fact that the legislature has a duty to establish the guarantees of mass media freedom by means of a law, stems from the Constitution'.[154]

178. Article 29 of the LPIP regulates fair competition in the field of provision of information to the public. In part 1 of the Article, it reiterates the constitutional norm (Article 44(2) of the Constitution): State and municipal agencies, as well as all types of other enterprises, agencies and organizations or natural persons may not monopolize the media.

---

153. The Supreme Council of Lithuania was the first representative organ of independent Lithuania. It functioned between 24 Feb. 1990 and 11 Nov. 1992 and was replaced by the Seimas. Initially elected as the Supreme Council of the Lithuanian Soviet Socialist Republic, it changed its name into the Supreme Council of Lithuania immediately after the Declaration of Restoration of Independent Lithuania was announced on 11 Mar. 1990. By the Declaration of 28 of November 1996, the Seimas has renamed it into the 'Supreme Council – Restoration Seimas' (lith. 'Aukščiausioji Taryba–Atkuriamasis Seimas').
154. Ruling of the Constitutional Court of 21 Dec. 2006.

179. Article 29(2) of the LPIP places an obligation on the State to create equal legal and economic conditions for fair competition among producers and disseminators of public information, except for producers and/or disseminators of productions of violent and erotic nature. It also states that under the procedure established by this Law and other laws, State and municipal institutions shall exercise control to uphold pluralism in the provision of information to the public and fair competition, avoiding the abuse of a dominant position by producers and/or disseminators of public information or in any separate segment of the media market.

180. According to the Constitutional Court, the provisions of Article 25 of the Constitution (paragraph 36) when construed together with the provisions of Paragraph 1 of Article 46 of the Constitution and other provisions of the Constitution, also express the constitutional principle of variety of sources of public information (paragraphs 29–32). All this implies that if the Constitution is heeded, a big part of the mass media market will always be held by private persons and a big part of the space of public information will be composed of information disseminated through private mass media.[155]

§2. Licensing Requirements

181. Article 22(6) sets out a legal person who may not be engaged in broadcasting activities. State and municipal institutions and establishments (except for scientific and educational institutions), banks, political parties may not be producers of public information and (or) their participants, but may publish non-periodical information publications, and have information society information media intended to inform the public about their activities unless otherwise provided by law.

182. Although all persons, except for the cases specified in laws, are free to produce and/or disseminate information in the Republic of Lithuania, broadcasting activity is subject to licencing. In view of this, the Constitutional Court has held that 'the state has a duty to control the use of electronic communication channels (radio frequencies) assigned to radio and television broadcasters and to regulate the conditions of the entering of broadcasters into the market and the concentration of the market' with the aim of guaranteeing the dissemination of information to the society.[156]

183. Broadcasting and retransmission licenses shall be issued by tender, except in certain cases. Accordingly, the LPIP sets out the types of TV and (or) radio broadcasting activity which can get the license without going through the procedure of public tender (Article 31(11)):

- broadcasting of radio programmes by a terrestrial radio station or a network of such stations;

155. Ruling of the Constitutional Court of 21 Dec. 2006.
156. *Ibid.*

- broadcasting of television programmes by a terrestrial television station or a network of such stations;
- broadcasting of television programmes by a cable television network;
- broadcasting of television programmes by the MMDS network;
- broadcasting of television programmes by electronic communications networks the main purpose of which is not broadcasting and/or re-broadcasting of radio and/or television programmes and/or programmes, except broadcasting of television programmes through the information society media (websites, webpages);
- broadcasting of television programmes by an artificial earth satellite (satellites).

184. Commission, in accordance with the procedure, laid down by the Rules for Licensing of Broadcasting Activities and Re-broadcast Content, issues licenses (Article 31(3)).

185. When issuing broadcasting licences, priority shall be given to persons who undertake to produce original cultural, informational and educational programmes, ensure accurate and impartial presentation of information, respect a person's dignity and right to privacy, protect minors from public information which might have a detrimental effect on their physical, mental and moral development as well as to persons who have undertaken to broadcast radio and/or television programmes that are not yet broadcast by other broadcasters of radio and/or television programmes within the designated reception zone (Article 31(9)).

186. According to Article 31(10) of the LPIP, broadcasting licences and licences of re-broadcast content are be issued under the tender procedure, except for the cases specified in Article 31(12). The licenses are issued without tender in the following cases:

- to research and higher education institutions or educational establishments – for broadcasting educational and cultural radio and/or television programmes by terrestrial radio and/or television stations with a power level ranging up to 20 W;
- for broadcasting television programmes by cable television networks;
- for broadcasting television programmes by electronic communications networks, the main purpose of which is not the broadcasting and/or re-broadcasting of radio and/or television programmes;
- for broadcasting television programmes by an artificial Earth satellite (satellites);
- in other cases, provided for in the plan for the assignment of radio frequencies for broadcasting and transmission of radio and television programmes.

187. Under Article 33(1) of the LPIP persons wishing to carry out an unlicensed activity of broadcasting radio and/or television programmes, re-broadcasters who will not use radio frequencies (channels) provided for in the plan for the assignment of radio frequencies for broadcasting and transmission of radio and television programmes, as well as persons providing users with the services of dissemination of television programmes and/or individual programmes via the Internet, providers of on-demand audiovisual media services must, before starting to carry out the said activity, notify the LRTK about this following the procedure laid down the Rules for Licensing of Broadcasting Activities and Re-broadcast Content. The persons may start carrying out unlicensed activities of broadcasting, re-broadcasting radio and/or television programmes, to provide users with the services of dissemination of television programmes and/or individual programmes via the Internet on the day following the submission of the notification to the Commission or on the day indicated in the notification if that day is later than the day of submission of the notification to the Commission.

188. The Minister of Culture of Lithuania upon advice by the LRTK adopts the rules on fixing the amount of annual fee for broadcasting and re-broadcasting of radio and/or television programmes, dissemination via the Internet or provision of on-demand audiovisual media services and based on the rules assesses the amount of the annual fee for the applicant. According to the Rules on fixing the amount of annual fee for broadcasting and re-broadcasting of radio and/or television programmes,[157] the fee is assessed considering the following criteria: the contents of the programmes (the lower fee shall be granted the more programmes of original culture, informational, educational nature and local news are disseminated), the territory covered by the licensee, the number of habitants residing in the covered territory (the higher the number of habitants, the higher annual fee) and the competition conditions in the territory (if other service providers are offering the same or similar services, the fee is lower). The LRT as the public broadcaster is subject to a lower annual fee – the amount of the fixed fee shall be multiplied by the coefficient of 0.01.

189. Lastly, the licence to translate, retranslate to the public, can be withdrawn from private persons with these conditions present:[158]

(1) LRTK suspends licence of licensee or LRT permit for three months if:

The Communications Regulatory Authority of the Republic of Lithuania (the CRA) revokes the right to use radio frequency and applies to the LRTK for the suspension of the license, LRT permit; they announce the confidential information specified in the Law and they have been already fined in accordance with the law or other sanctions provided for the same violation within last 12 months; they violate main conditions of the broadcasting license or retransmitted license, LRT permit and/or obligations regarding the broadcast and/or retransmitted radio and/or television program and for the last 12 months for the same violation he had repeatedly been given an administrative penalty; they fail to comply with the decision of the LRTK and he gets the same fine or other sanctions provided in the Law after repeated violation;

157. The Resolution of the Minister of Culture of 21 Apr. 2011 No IV-318 'Regarding the approval of the description of the procedure for determining the amount of the annual fee for a broadcasting and retransmission license'.

158. The Resolution of the Minister of Culture of 12 Apr. 2011 No. 44-2096 On the Approval of Licensing Rules for Broadcasting and Retransmission Activities Arts 54, 55.

they do not pay the fine imposed on the basis of the Law for three months; they violate the requirements of law on protection of minors from negative impact on public information on their physical, mental, moral development and has been repeatedly imposed an administrative penalty for the same violation during 12 months; the licensee fails to pay the annual fee on time (LRT works on state budget); the licensee does not pay the fees established by the Law to finance the activities of the LRTK and he has been issued two warnings for the same violation during the last 24 months.

(2) LRTK withdraws license completely if a licensee or LRT:

refuses the license or LRT – it's permit; is being liquidated or reorganized; more than 2 months in a row, or more than 3 months throughout a calendar year does not carry out broadcasting activities (without the consent of the LRTK) provided in the license, LRT permit; does not broadcast or retransmit radio or television programmes on the frequencies under the conditions specified in the license or permit; did not start the broadcasting activity according to the broadcasting license; has provided incorrect data for the broadcasting license, permit or license for retransmitted content; does not eliminate the violation for which the temporary suspension of the license or permit was issued, or within 12 months after the suspension of the license or permit commits the same violation; without the consent of LRTK, due to the transfer of shares, or changes in the management of the licensee, or in the application incorrect data is stated to obtain the consent of LRTK; the Communications Regulatory Authority of the Republic of Lithuania (CRA) revokes the right to use radio frequency and applies to the Commission for the revocation of the license, permit.

§3. Publicity Requirements

190. Legal persons who are the managers of media dissemination means have the duty to inform the Ministry of Culture about the identity of the owners of the legal person, whose share is at least 10% (paragraph 36). Such information is made public on the Internet site of the Ministry of Culture (Article 24(1) of LPIP). This clause does not apply to the producers of information.

191. The President of the Republic of Lithuania, the members of Seimas, the Government, the councils of municipalities, public officers of political reliance, heads of the state and municipal institutions must inform the Ministry of Culture about their participation in the ownership or management of media dissemination means. Such information is also made public on the Internet site of the Ministry of Culture (Article 24(2) of LPIP). This clause does not apply to the producers of information.

192. However, the norms set out in Article 24(1) and 24(2) lack effectiveness due to the difficulties to control the veracity of the submitted information. It shall also be mentioned that all producers and disseminators of information, as well as their owners, are subject to the duty to provide information in the mass media about the donations exceeding 10 basic social benefits,[159] disclosing the amount received and the source.

159. As of 1 Jan. 2021 one basic social benefit amounts to EUR 40.

Chapter 3. Programme Standards

193. Programme standards are formulated in LPIP. They apply to both the public broadcaster and private broadcasters.

194. First, paragraphs 2 and 3 of Article 3 of LPIP set out:

- Producers and disseminators of public information as well as journalists and publishers in their activities shall be governed by the Constitution, laws and international treaties of the Republic of Lithuania, also by the principles of humanism, equality, tolerance and respect for every human being; they shall respect freedom of speech, creativity, religion and conscience, and the diversity of opinion, adhere to the norms of professional ethics and the provisions of the Code of Ethics in Providing Information to the Public of Lithuania ..., contribute to the development of democracy and public openness, promote the civic society and state progress, enhance the state independence and nurture the state language, national culture and morality.
- Public information must be presented in the media in a fair, accurate and impartial manner.

195. Also, all broadcasts must respect basic human rights, including human dignity (Article 13) and private life (Article 14 of LPIP). Pieces of literature, scientific, artistic and other works shall be used in conformity with the Law on Copyright and Related Rights as well as other laws and legal acts (Article 21 of the same Law).

196. In its ruling of 21 December 2006, Constitutional Court[160] held that greater requirements are raised for radio and television than for other means of mass media. Moreover, that the specific character of radio and television as a means of mass media increases the responsibility of the public broadcaster even more. The biggest requirements of mass media ethics must be applied to the public broadcaster (to its programmes and broadcasts). For example, dissemination of any disinformation (which, as mentioned before, is not covered by the constitutional concept of freedom of information) is prohibited in programmes and broadcasts of the public broadcaster (as well as in those of other broadcasters).

§1. Impartiality

197. As stated above, by paragraph 3 of Article 3 of LPIP both the public broadcaster and private broadcasters are subject to the duty to present public information in a fair, accurate, and impartial manner.

198. Article 22(11) of the same Law adds that producers and/or disseminators of public information in disseminating information to the public, may not distort

160. Ruling of the Constitutional Court of 21 Dec. 2006 'On the status, management and rights of the national broadcaster.

correct and impartial information and opinions and use that for sordid purposes. Public information shall not be compatible with journalistic campaigns which are based on prejudice or have the aim to satisfy group or political interests. They must also be objective and impartial and provide as many opinions as possible on the controversial issues relating to politics, economy and other issues of public life.

199. The duty of the public broadcaster to be guided by the principle of impartiality is also repeated in Article 3(1) of the LNRT defining the mission of the public service broadcasting. The guarantee of this principle by the public broadcaster is its' impartiality from the State. It is achieved by private broadcasters, ensuring fair competition in the field of broadcasting.

200. A very important guarantee of impartiality of all broadcasters is the prohibition binding every person, whether private or public, individual or legal, to exert pressure on the producer or disseminator of public information, their participant or a journalist to compel them to present information in the media in an incorrect and biased manner (Article 7 of the LPIP).

§2. Cultural Diversity

201. In its ruling of 8 July 2005, the Constitutional Court held that the state is constitutionally obliged to support and foster culture as a national value of universal importance – the material and spiritual creative activity and its results that should be transferred to future generations. According to the Constitution, the state must, by its positive decisions (inter alia, legal regulation), encourage and support by using state funds and other resources for the creation, spreading, propagation and preserving material and spiritual cultural values. The freedom of accessibility to cultural values is entrenched in the Constitution, which is related also with the imperative of an open society: if this freedom is not ensured, the striving for an open society would suffer damage as well.[161]

202. In the ruling of 21 December 2006, the Constitutional Court stated that the state can choose various ways of dissemination of the said information through radio and television, i.e. to render corresponding public services to the public in various ways. It can do so not only through the broadcaster established by the state but also through private radio and television broadcasters, but entrust various radio and television broadcasters with broadcasting (by following corresponding requirements) certain public radio and television programmes. The state can guarantee the interest of society to be informed also by entrusting (tendering) dissemination of public programmes to those radio and television broadcasters, who would ensure the implementation of the said interest in the most efficient manner.[162]

161. Ruling of the Constitutional Court of 8 Jul. 2005.
162. Ruling of the Constitutional Court of 21 Dec. 2006.

203. Considering such understanding of the Constitutional norms, the public broadcaster is under the duty to 'acquaint the public with the variety of European and world culture, fundamentals of the current civilization …, create, nurture and protect the values of national culture' (Article 3(1) of the LNRT); the programmes of the LRT shall reflect the plurality of topics and genres (Article 4(1) of the LNRT).

204. According to Article 3(2) of LPIP, all producers and disseminators of public information, as well as journalists and publishers, are subject to the duty of respecting the diversity of opinion.

205. Article 40 of LPIP regulates the promotion of European works in the course of the provision of on-demand audiovisual media services. Paragraph 1 of the article sets out that providers of on-demand audiovisual media services falling under the jurisdiction of the Republic of Lithuania shall promote, where practicable and by appropriate means, the production of and access to European works. Paragraph 2 provides for that in pursuing the activities specified in paragraph 1 of this article, providers of on-demand audiovisual media services shall ensure that at least half of the programmes in the catalogue of on-demand audiovisual media services are European works.

§3. Linguistic Requirements

206. According to Article 34(1) of LPIP, information shall be produced and disseminated in the state language or any other language according to the legal regulation – the Law on the State Language, LPIP, as well as the resolutions of the State Commission on the Lithuanian Language. Producers and disseminators of public information, in cooperation with the competent state and municipal institutions and agencies, shall, where possible, ensure that the disseminated public information is accessible to the disabled.

207. Article 34(2) of LPIP sets out that radio and/or television programmes broadcast in a language other than Lithuanian must be translated into Lithuanian or shown with Lithuanian subtitles, except for educational, occasional, special, music and re-broadcast foreign radio and/or television programmes or parts of programmes as well as programmes produced by broadcasters of radio and/or television programmes intended for the ethnic minorities. The requirements whether the programmes broadcast in a language other than Lithuanian must be translated into Lithuanian or shown with Lithuanian subtitles depends on the origin of the language:

- programmes broadcast in a foreign language which is one of the EU languages, must be translated into Lithuanian or shown with Lithuanian subtitles;
- programmes broadcast in a foreign language which is not one of the EU languages, the overall duration of which does not exceed ninety minutes a day, must be translated into Lithuanian or shown with Lithuanian subtitles;

– when the duration of the programmes broadcast in a foreign language which is not one of the EU languages exceeds ninety minutes a day, it must be translated into Lithuanian.

208. Such complex regulation was introduced in the law to regulate the length of the programmes originating from countries other than the EU.

209. Article 34(3) of LPIP forbids broadcasters of television programmes from showing audiovisual works which have been translated from an official EU language into a non-EU language.

210. Article 34(4) of the same law provides that when re-broadcasting television programmes, re-broadcasters and/or other persons providing services of dissemination of television programmes or individual programmes via the Internet for users of the Republic of Lithuania must give priority to the official EU languages. Television programmes in the official languages of the EU must comprise at least 90% of the programmes. This requirement does not apply to television programme packages disseminated for additional payment. However, where there is a possibility to choose between the official EU language or any other language, the EU language shall be used.

211. Concerning the public broadcaster, Article 4(4) of the LNRT indicates that audiovisual works of art in a foreign language shall be translated into Lithuanian language or subtitled. The Council of the LRT shall establish a proportion of audiovisual works of art in a foreign language to be translated into Lithuanian language or subtitled.

§4. Protection of Minors (Indecency and Violence)

212. Minors[163] are granted protection by the Constitution. Article 39(3) sets out that minors shall be protected by law.

213. The Law on the Fundamentals of Protection of the Rights of the Child provides some basic guidance on the protection of children[164] against public information having a detrimental effect on them.

214. Article 17 of LPIP provides that:

– Producers and/or disseminators of public information must, in accordance with the procedure established by law, ensure that minors are protected from public

163. Minors are persons under 18 years of age (Art. 2.5(1) of the Civil Code, Art. 2(3) of the Law of the Republic of Lithuania on the Protection of Minors against the Detrimental Effect of Public Information).

164. According to the Law on the Fundamentals of Protection of the Rights of the Child, child is a human being below the age of 18 years (Art. 11).

information which might have a detrimental effect on their physical, mental or moral development, in particular public information that involves the dissemination of information of pornographic and/or violent nature and information encouraging addictions.
- The criteria for assigning public information to the information which has a detrimental effect on the physical, mental or moral development of minors shall be established in the Law of the Republic of Lithuania on the Protection of Minors against the Detrimental Effect of Public (DEPI).
- Establishes the criteria of public information, which might cause physical, mental or moral detriment to the development of minors, the procedure of making available such information to the public and the rights, obligations and liability of the producers, disseminators and their owners, journalists and institutions regulating their activities. The Law applies to information disseminated through media and other channels, i.e. advertising, self-advertising (trailers), trademarks, computer games and other public information (Article 8(1)).

215. According to Article 4(1) of the mentioned law, public information that causes physical, mental or moral detriment to the development of minors is information:

- which relates to the portrayal of physical or psychological violence: when the killing, mutilation or torture of people and animals are portrayed in detail, also vandalism, a positive assessment of violence and coercion or cruelty are being indulged;
- which displays a dead or cruelly mutilated body of a person, except in cases when such a portrayal is necessary for identification purposes;
- which is erotic: when sexual desire is aroused, sexual intercourse or an imitation thereof or other sexual gratification and genitals and sex paraphernalia are displayed;
- which arouses fear or horror;
- in which addiction to drugs, psychotropic substances, tobacco or alcohol, is favourably assessed and the use, production, distribution or acquisition thereof is promoted;
- which encourages self-mutilation or suicide;
- in which criminal activity is assessed favourably or criminals are idealized;
- which is related to the imitation of criminal activity;
- which contains incitement to discrimination based on nationality, race, gender, origin, disability, sexual orientation, religion or other affiliation;
- in which obscene language, words and gestures are frequently employed.

216. Nowadays it is important to mention that according to DEPI, any information that encourages the concept of entering into a marriage and creation of a family other than stipulated in (the Constitution Article 38 and Civil Code (Articles 3.12–3.17) has a detrimental effect on minors. That means, any other public information that paints, involuntary marriage, marriage when either of the spouses is underage, marriage between close relatives, polygamous marriages, and same-sex marriage in a positive light, is a violation of Lithuanian law.

217. According to Article 6 of the law, the following public information is also considered to cause detrimental effects to the development of minors:

- information about criminal activities or other violations of the law; minors who are not hiding from the law enforcement institutions, or who have been the victim of a criminal action or other violations of the law, based on which, his/her identity could be established;
- information making public of the personal data of a minor who has mutilated themselves or has attempted this has committed suicide or has attempted it, according to which, their personal identity may be established;
- information about a minor whereby their dignity is degraded and (or) their interests are violated;
- instances when in misuse of minors' reliance and inexperience their opinions and evaluations are presented in a context of negative social phenomena;
- instances when photos or filmed material concerning minors are presented in a context of negative social phenomena when their identity could be established.

218. Information that causes physical, mental, or moral detriment to the development of minors may not be disseminated directly to the minors. Such information may be made available to the public only in places where access of the minors is restricted or at a time of day when minors do not become exposed to it, or when there are technical means for the persons responsible for the minors to restrict the spread of the information to the minors.

219. Programmes containing information, that causes physical, mental or moral detriment to the development of minors may be broadcasted without using the technical means if they are properly indexed and broadcasted at the appropriate time of the day, such information:

- shall be indexed 'S'[165] and may be broadcasted from 23.00 p.m. to 6.00 a.m.;
- shall be indexed 'N-14' and may be broadcasted from 21.00 p.m. to 6.00 a.m. when information contained in them negatively affects minors under 14 years of age;
- shall be indexed 'N-7' when information contained in them negatively affects minors under 7 years of age.

220. A different index is established for movies in the Law on Cinema[166] (Article 14(10)):

- index 'V' shall be used for movies intended for all age groups;
- index 'N-7' – for movies intended for children older than 7 years of age;
- index 'N-13' – for movies intended for children older than 13 years of age;
- index 'N-16' – for movies intended for children older than 16 years of age;
- index 'N-18' – for movies intended for adults.

165. The index 'S' comes from the Lithuanian word 'Suaugęs' meaning 'Adult'.
166. Official Gazette, 27-03-2002, No. 31-1107.

221. The Inspector of Journalist Ethics is responsible for the exercise of supervision over the implementation of the provisions of the DEPI (Article 9(1)). The Inspector is supported by other institutions working within the scope of their competence: the Council of the LRT, the LRTK of Lithuania, the Ministry of Culture, the Lithuanian Ethics Commission of Journalists and Publishers, the Office of the Ombudsman for the Protection of the Rights of the Child, governing institutions of municipalities, the Information Society Development Committee, CRA and the Police Department under the Ministry of the Interior (Article 9(7)).

222. Through the Law, the Inspector is responsible for the supervision of the protection of minors against the information having a detrimental effect. Though according to the law wide range of measures is at the disposal of the Inspector – from the warning of the accountable person for the violation of the Law to the application of administrative liability penalties – it is argued that the law is not effective in practice due to the difficulties of application of liability.[167]

§5. Human Dignity

223. Human dignity is the fundamental principle of the Constitution. Article 21 of the Constitution sets out:

- The person of the human being shall be inviolable.
- The dignity of the human being shall be protected by law.

224. Article 3(1) of the LNRT which is aimed at defining the mission of the public service broadcasting inter alia states that 'human dignity and human rights must be respected in the broadcasts, and the principles of morality and ethics must not be violated'. A special rule dealing with human dignity concerns advertising and commercial audiovisual announcements. According to Article 39(1) of LPIP, they shall not violate human dignity.

225. Article 10(1) of the Law on the Fundamentals of Protection of the Rights of the Child sets out that every child has the right to human dignity.

226. The duty to respect human dignity is repeated in the laws regulating mass media. Article 19(2) of the LPIP provides that 'It shall be prohibited to disseminate disinformation and information which is slanderous and offensive to a person or which degrades his honour and dignity'. A person whose human dignity has been offended in the mass media has the right to reply (Articles 15 and 44).

227. Article 13(1) of LPIP sets out the requirements for the protection of the basic human rights, honour and dignity:

167. L Meškauskaitė, *Žiniasklaidos teisė, 2-as leidimas* [*Media Law*, 2nd ed.], Vilnius: Vilniaus universiteto Teisės fakultetas, 2018, 108, 110.

– To avoid violation of a person's rights and to protect his honour and dignity, in collecting and publishing information, it shall be prohibited:
– to film, photograph, make audio and video recordings without a person's consent within the residential premises of the natural person, the private domain of the natural person and a fenced or otherwise clearly marked territory belonging thereto, regardless of whether that person is present in the aforementioned places;
– to film, photograph or make audio and video recordings during non-public events without the consent of organizers who have the right to hold such events;
– to film and photograph a person and use his images for advertising purposes in the media without the consent of that person;
– to film and photograph a person with evident physical handicaps without that person's consent or to film and photograph a person in a helpless state due to a health impairment;
– to film or photograph a child or to make audio and video recordings of him without the consent of at least one of the parents, guardians or custodians and the child himself. It shall be prohibited to use photographs, audio or video recordings of children in the information of erotic, pornographic and violent nature;
– to film or photograph close-ups of a deceased or fatal casualty without the consent of the family members of the deceased or the fatal casualty or to make video recordings of him.

228. The producer and disseminator of information shall respect and protect the right to privacy in cases of death and illness, shall not mention personal data in cases of suicide or suicide attempts, as well as not mention motives and means of suicide or suicide attempts, shall not imply suicide as a means of solving problems or as mundane, acceptable fact, shall not romanticize suicides, shall not show suicide process or a person in an attempt to commit suicide, or who has committed suicide. In news about suicide or an attempt of suicide the producer and disseminator of information shall present information about emotional and psychological help groups and self-help groups.[168]

§6. Right of Reply

229. The right of reply has been dealt with above (paragraphs 101–103). Here the special rules concerning broadcasting shall be mentioned.

230. The LPIP contains the rule concerning the media.[169]

–Any natural person whose honour and dignity have been degraded by false, inaccurate or biased information published about him in the media, also any legal

168. Article 22(11) of LPIP.

169. Media is a newspaper, journal, bulletin or any other publication, a book, television programme, radio programme, film or any other production of audio and video studios, the information society media and any other media used for public dissemination of information (Art. 2(86) of the Law on Provision of Information to the Public).

person whose professional reputation or other legitimate interests have been damaged by false, inaccurate or biased information shall have the right of reply, refuting the false information or correcting the published information, or shall have the right to require that the producer and/or disseminator of public information issue a refutation of false information in accordance with the procedure established in Article 44 of this Law.

231. According to Article 44 of LPIP affected person shall send a written request specifying which published information contradicts reality, when and where it was announced, which statements of the published information degrade the honour and dignity of the natural person or damage the professional reputation of the legal person, and demanding that the media which disseminated such information published the refutation.

232. The refutation shall be published free of charge of the same size and in the same form (or by any other adequate means) as the false information degrading human dignity (legal person's reputation) within two weeks, except for the media the periodicity of which is less frequent. In that case, the refutation shall be published within two weeks in the first programme of the public broadcaster (the LRT) and the first publication or programme of the media after the receipt of the refutation, without comments, in the same place, of the same size and in the same form (television and radio – on the same day of the week and at the same time) as the false information degrading human dignity (legal person's reputation). The same requirements apply to cases where the media, of their own free will, decides to publish the refutation. The media must publish the response regardless of whether the information damaging human dignity (or a legal person's reputation) was disseminated on behalf of the media or any other person.

233. In case of denial to publish refutation, the media shall reply to a person within two weeks indicating the reasons and motives for refusal.

234. Refusal to publish or otherwise announce the refutation in the manner prescribed by LPIP may be appealed against in court according to the place of residence (place of registration) of the claimant. A complaint must be examined not later than within 30 days (including non-working days) of its lodgement.

§7. Other Requirements

235. Article 22(11) of LPIP besides requirements of impartiality and respect for human dignity discussed above (paragraphs 197–200, 228) sets out some other requirements. Producer and disseminator of information shall not propagate or portray attractively smoking, consuming alcohol or narcotic substances.

236. According to the same article, producer and disseminator of information shall not propagate people or groups of people engaged in supernatural, surreal, paranormal activity, except for the cases when such information is presented with the aim of amusement or as an object of investigation. Implication shall not be made in the information that astrologers, palmists, chiromants, extrasens, bioenergetics may advice about future, health, money, etc.

Chapter 4. Political Broadcasting

§1. Rules on Political Independence of Broadcasters

237. Political independence of broadcasters is one of the guarantees of a democratic society.

238. Both public broadcasters and private broadcasters shall remain politically independent. This is sought by various means.

239. Although the LRT, the public broadcaster, is established by the State, it is an independent legal body. The Constitutional Court has stressed that 'the law must establish such model of governance of the public broadcaster, which would ensure that one will not deviate from the constitutional mission of the public broadcaster, also that independence of the public broadcaster will not be denied'.[170] The current managing system of the LRT shall guarantee its political independence – the Council as the institution entrusted with the main managing competence within the LRT is composed of the representatives of the entire society and the Director is appointed by the Council through a public tender procedure. To guarantee the political independence of the public broadcaster the Members of the Seimas, Government and the LRTK may not become members of the Council (Article 9(4) of the LNRT). Having the same aim the director who was a member of a political party shall suspend his/her membership for the term of office (Article 12(3) of the LNRT). However, as it was stated above,[171] Lithuanian authors argue that the formation procedure of the Council and the length of term (6 years) do not fully meet the principle of political independence.

240. In the same Ruling of 21 December 2006 the Constitutional Court has emphasized that financing of the public broadcaster from several sources is one of the most important guarantees of its political independence. Therefore, the Constitutional Court concluded that the possibility of income of the public broadcaster from commercial advertising is not in contradiction with the Constitution. As stated above,[172] the financing system of the LRT has been changed since 2015 and commercial broadcasting was banned. However, no indications are suggesting the current financing system is in contradiction with the principle of political independence of the LRT.

241. According to Article 22(8) of LPIP applicable to all media, it bans state and municipal institutions and agencies (except for higher education and research institutions and educational establishments), also legal persons whose founder, unitholder or shareholder is the State or municipality, its institution or agency, and political parties from becoming producers of public information either directly or indirectly (e.g. becoming the participant of the producers of public information).

170. Ruling of the Constitutional Court of 21 Dec. 2006.
171. See above at no. 153.
172. See above at nos 165, 167.

242. According to Article 22(11) of LPIP media shall not satisfy political interests and the plurality of opinions shall be presented.

§2. Fair Representation in Election Periods and Political Advertising

243. The Law on Advertising does not regulate political advertising (Article 1(5)). It was not until 2004 when political advertising was regulated in the Law on Funding of, and Control over Funding of, Political Campaigns. However, the law does not distinguish between political advertising and the rules guaranteeing fair representation in the election periods as all these rules follow under the notion of 'political advertising'.

244. Special rules deal with the fair representation of political parties in election (referendum) periods. The Law on Advertising[173] is not applicable to political advertising (Article 1(5) on the Law on Advertising). The dissemination of political advertising is regulated by the Law on Elections,[174] the Law on Referendum, and the Law on Funding of, and Control over Funding of, Political Campaigns.[175]

245. The special rules aim to guarantee the equality of political parties in elections. Thus, a public service broadcaster must grant free of charge airtime for the discussion of the candidates during their participation in elections. The Central Electoral Commission is responsible for the rules governing such broadcasts.

246. Political advertising during a political campaign must be marked by indicating the source of funding and visibly separated from other disseminated information.[176]

247. Public information producers or disseminators may disseminate political advertising only at the rates and under the conditions which are equal to all political campaign participants and which are submitted to the Central Electoral Commission. The rates and conditions of political advertising applicable during a political campaign may not be presented or changed during the political campaign. The rates and conditions of political advertising are applicable no later than until a political campaign may be changed with the consent of the Central Electoral Commission. The Central Electoral Commission shall immediately announce the rates on its website.[177]

248. At all times it is prohibited to disseminate political advertising:[178]

173. Official Gazette 2013, No. 57-2854 (01-06-2013), code 1131010ISTA0XII-315.
174. The Law on Elections to the Seimas, the Law on Elections to Municipal Councils, the Law on Presidential Elections, and the Law on Elections to European Parliament.
175. Official Gazette 2004, No. 135-4894, code 1041010ISTA0IX-2428, new version No. XII-615, 26-11-2013, Official Gazette 2013, No. 128-6514 (14-12-2013), code 1131010ISTA0XII-615.
176. Article 15 of the Law on Funding of, and Control over Funding of, Political Campaigns.
177. Article 16(4) of the Law on Funding of, and Control over Funding of, Political Campaigns.
178. Article 16(1) of the Law on Funding of, and Control over Funding of, Political Campaigns.

– on the front page of a periodical;
– if the dissemination of such advertising violates of the Constitution and laws of the Republic of Lithuania.

249. Besides these restrictions, during an election (referendum) period it is prohibited:[179]

– to disseminate political advertising free of charge, except discussion programmes,
– in television, except discussion programmes and campaigning-related videos of not less than 30 seconds duration in which a political campaign participant informs about their political programme or speaks on issues topical to the public.

250. All laws on elections (referendum) contain norms on prohibition to take advantage of one's official position for election campaigning.[180]

251. The following shall not be regarded as political advertising:[181]

– information disseminated during the period other than a political campaign about activities of state politicians, political parties, their management bodies, except for the cases where such notices agitate to vote in the interest of the state politician, political party or its candidate during a future political campaign, or remuneration is provided for such notices, or remuneration is envisaged;
– information notices of usual character disseminated free of charge during a political campaign about activities of state politicians, political parties, candidates, as well as information which refrains from inciting non-participation in a referendum, voting for or against the adoption of a decision submitted for the referendum.

§3. News and Current Affairs Programmes

252. Television advertisements and teleshopping may not feature individuals who regularly present news programmes, nor they may be dubbed by such persons (Article 39(10) of LPIP).

253. Newscasts are only allowed to be interrupted for each scheduled period of at least thirty minutes once for television advertising and (or) teleshopping (item 7 of Article 39(10) of LPIP).

179. Article 16(2) of the Law on Funding of, and Control over Funding of, Political Campaigns.
180. Article 47 of the Law on Presidential Elections, Art. 54 of the Law on Elections to the Seimas, Art. 51 of the Law on Elections to Municipal Councils, Art. 18(10) of the Law on Elections to European Parliament.
181. Article 16(6) of the Law on Funding of, and Control over Funding of, Political Campaigns.

254. News programmes may not be sponsored (Article 40(4) of the Law on Provision of Information to the Public). Product placement is not allowed in news programmes (Article 40^1(4) LPIP).

Chapter 5. Advertising Rules

§1. VARIOUS FORMS OF COMMERCIAL COMMUNICATIONS

255. The Law on Advertising regulates advertising in the Republic of Lithuania. In Article 2(8) it sets out the definition of advertising: it is information disseminated in any form and by any means and relating to a person's commercial and economic, financial or professional activities, where it promotes the purchase of goods or use of services, including the purchase of immovable property and the takeover of property rights and obligations. According to this definition, remuneration is not a criterion of advertising.[182]

256. Lithuanian legal scholars argue that there are four types of advertising: commercial, cultural, social and political.[183] The laws do not use the concept of cultural advertising, while the concept of social advertising is used only scarcely.

257. The Law on Advertising does not regulate political and social advertising, as well as announcements not connected with commercial, financial or professional activity (Article 1(5)). Advertising on TV is also regulated by the LPIP.

258. Misleading advertising is advertising which in any way, including its presentation, deceives or is likely to deceive the persons to whom it is addressed or whom it reaches and which, by reason of its deceptive nature, is likely to affect their economic behaviour or which, for those reasons, injures or is likely to injure another person's opportunities to compete (Article 2(3)).

259. Comparative advertising means advertising which explicitly or by implication identifies a competitor of the supplier of advertising or the goods or services offered by the competitor (Article 2(4)).

260. Surreptitious advertising means information disseminated in any form and by any means about a producer of goods or a provider of services, the name or the activities thereof, the trademark presented in a way that may confuse advertising consumers as to the actual purpose of presentation of such advertising. Such presentation of information shall be considered as surreptitious advertising in all cases if it is done in return for payment or for similar consideration (Article 2(5)).

---

182. L. Meškauskaitė, *Žiniasklaidos teisė, 2-as leidimas* [*Media Law*, 2nd ed.], Vilnius: Vilniaus universiteto Teisės fakultetas, 2018, 255–256; L. Markauskas, Reklamos teisinis reglamentavimas: teorija ir praktika [Regulation of Advertising: Theory and Practice], Vilnius: Mokesčių srautas, 2008, 24.

183. L. Meškauskaitė, *Žiniasklaidos teisė, 2-as leidimas* [*Media Law*, 2nd ed.], Vilnius: Vilniaus universiteto Teisės fakultetas, 2018, 259.

261. Teleshopping means direct offers broadcast to the public by a broadcaster of television programmes to purchase goods or use services, including offers to purchase immovable property, property rights and obligations, in return for payment (Article 2(66) of the LPIP).

262. Teleshopping window means a programme intended for teleshopping inserts broadcast in television programmes that are not exclusively intended for teleshopping (Article 2(67) of the LPIP).

§2. Restrictions on Content

263. The most important principles of advertising are: advertising shall be proper and accurate and clearly recognizable (Article 3 on the Law of Advertising).

264. Article 4(1) of the Law on Advertising sets out that advertising is subject to the requirements of the Law on the State Language.

265. The following advertising is prohibited by Article 4(2) on the Law of Advertising: that violates principles of public morality, degrades human honour and dignity, incites national, racial, religious, gender-related or social hatred and discrimination as well as defames or misinforms, promotes coercion and aggression and gives rise to panic, promotes behaviour which poses a threat to health, security and the environment, abuses superstitions, people's trust and their lack of experience or knowledge, makes a reference to the name and surname of a natural person without their consent, presents their opinion, information about their private or public life and property and makes use of the natural person's image, uses special subliminal means and technologies in advertising dissemination, uses advertising material which has been prepared in violation of copyright to works of literature, art and science and/or related rights, scorns religious symbols of the religious communities registered in Lithuania.

266. A great example of such a prohibition is a case that went even to the European Court of Justice – *Sekmadienis v. Lithuania.*[184]

267. In September and October 2012, for about two weeks, the applicant company ran an advertising campaign introducing a clothing line. The campaign featured three visual advertisements which were displayed on twenty advertising hoardings in public areas in Vilnius and on R.K.'s website (hereinafter 'the advertisements').

- The first of the three advertisements showed a young man with long hair, a headband, a halo around his head and several tattoos wearing a pair of jeans. A caption at the bottom of the image read 'Jesus, what trousers!' (liet. *Jėzau, kokios tavo kelnės!*).

184. https://hudoc.echr.coe.int/fre#{%22itemid%22:[%22001-180506%22]}.

- The second advertisement showed a young woman wearing a white dress and a headdress with white and red flowers in it. She had a halo around her head and was holding a string of beads. The caption at the bottom of the image read 'Dear Mary, what a dress!' (liet. *Marija brangi, kokia suknelė!*).
- The third advertisement showed the man and the woman together, wearing the same clothes and accessories as in the previous advertisements. The man was reclining and the woman was standing next to him with one hand placed on his head and the other on his shoulder. The caption at the bottom of the image read 'Jesus [and] Mary, what are you wearing!' (liet. *Jėzau Marija, kuo čia apsirengę!*).

268. And although these phrases could be considered as emotional interjection which is common in spoken Lithuanian, similar to 'oh my God!', 'oh Lord!', 'God forbid!' it still uses catholic symbols, which are not tolerated by the religious community. Given all the details, the European Court of Human rights decided that there was a violation of Article 10 of The Convention for the Protection of Human Rights and Fundamental Freedoms – freedom of expression.

269. Article 39(1) of LPIP states that information which degrades human dignity, promotes any discrimination based on race, sex or ethnic origin, nationality, citizenship, religion or belief, disability or age, contains manifestations or promotion of sexual orientation, is offensive to religious or political convictions or promotes behaviour prejudicial to health or safety or behaviour grossly prejudicial to the protection of the environment is prohibited.

270. Misleading advertising is prohibited in Lithuania (Article 5 of the Law on Advertising and Article 39(2), 39(11)(1) of the LPIP). Comparative advertising is subject to special requirements set out in Article 6 of the Law on Advertising.

271. Advertising and audiovisual commercial communications may not have a detrimental effect on the mental health of minors, their physical, mental or moral development (Article 4(4) of LPIP, also Article 7 on the Law on Advertising).

272. Surreptitious advertising is prohibited (Article 8(1) of the Law on Advertising, Article 39(5) of LPIP). Advertising must be clearly identifiable according to its form of presentation. Where there exists the likelihood that due to the form of presentation, consumers of advertising may not identify the advertising disseminated in the media, such advertising must be marked with the word 'advertisement' (Article 8(2) of the Law on Advertising).

273. According to the Law on Advertising it is prohibited to advertise goods, services or activity which is unlawful (Article 9).

274. Advertising of certain goods and services fall under special regulation, e.g. food (Article 14 on the Law on Advertising), medical services and goods (Article

15 on the Law on Advertising). Advertising of weapons and ammunition is permitted only at their points of sale, exhibitions of weapons and ammunition and publications intended for professionals (Article 16 on the Law on Advertising). Advertising of cosmetic products shall conform to the provisions of Regulation (EC) No. 1223/2009 of the European Parliament and of the Council of 30 November 2009 (Article 17 on the Law on Advertising). Advertising of biocidal products shall conform to the provisions of Regulation (EU) No. 528/2012 of the European Parliament and of the Council of 22 December 2012 concerning the making available on the market and use of biocidal products (Article 18 on the Law on Advertising).

275. Advertising of alcohol and tobacco products is banned in the Republic of Lithuania (Article 29(1) of the Law on Alcohol Control and Article 17(1) of the Law on Control of Tobacco, Tobacco Products and Related Products).

276. Persons regularly hosting news programmes may neither take part in advertising or audiovisual commercial communications nor voice them over (Article 39(10) of LPIP).

277. The standard of average consumer is used to judge whether advertising conforms to the requirements set out in the laws.[185] The concept of average consumer is not defined in laws and thus is defined by courts based on the case law of the CJEU.[186]

§3. Time and Frequency Restrictions

278. Article 39(11) of LPIP sets out quantitative rules for commercial communications, such as daily or hourly limits to advertising, special rules for insertion of advertising in programmes, the maximum number of interruptions, special categories of programmes which cannot be interrupted for advertising. The same goes for television advertising, announcement or teleshopping – they may not be inserted during religious services and religious programmes.

279. Television advertising and teleshopping must be inserted in programmes in blocks and containing at least two television advertising and/or teleshopping spots during one insertion. One television advertisement or one teleshopping may be inserted in a programme in transmissions of sports events or in other exceptional cases established by the Commission. The total time of television advertising spots and teleshopping spots within a given clock hour must not exceed 20%. This

185. L. Meškauskaitė, *Žiniasklaidos teisė, 2-as leidimas* [*Media Law*, 2nd ed.], Vilnius: Vilniaus universiteto Teisės fakultetas, 2018, 265.
186. L. Meškauskaitė, *Žiniasklaidos teisė, 2-as leidimas* [*Media Law*, 2nd ed.], Vilnius: Vilniaus universiteto Teisės fakultetas, 2018, 265.

requirement does not apply to the programmes broadcast by the broadcaster of television programmes itself and announcements of the ancillary products directly related to those programmes, sponsorship announcements and product placements.

280. Television advertising spots and/or teleshopping spots during sports or other events containing natural breaks must be inserted only during the natural breaks of such events. The broadcasting of films made for television (excluding series, serials and documentaries), cinematographic works and news programmes may be interrupted by television advertising and/or teleshopping once for each scheduled period of at least thirty minutes. The broadcasting of children's programmes may be interrupted by television advertising and/or teleshopping once for each scheduled period of at least thirty minutes, provided that the scheduled duration of the programme is greater than thirty minutes.

281. Teleshopping windows must be of a minimum uninterrupted duration of fifteen minutes. The number of teleshopping windows broadcasts per day may not exceed eight. Their total duration shall not exceed three hours per day. Teleshopping windows must be clearly distinguished from other programmes by optical and spatial means.

282. It is prohibited to insert advertising and/or teleshopping in re-broadcast television programmes or their parts.

§4. Sponsorship

283. Sponsorship means any contribution made by a person not engaged in the broadcasting of radio programmes and/or providing audiovisual media services and/or in the production of audiovisual or audio works to the financing of audiovisual media services and/or programmes with a view to promoting their name, trademark, image, activities or their products or services (Article 2(58) of LPIP).

284. Sponsorship in media is subject to special rules. Article 40 of LPIP sets out that media that are sponsored must meet the following requirements:

– their content and, in the case of broadcasting of television and/or radio programmes, their scheduling may in no circumstances be influenced in such a way as to affect the editorial responsibility and independence of the audiovisual media service provider and the broadcaster of radio programmes;
– they may not directly encourage the purchase or rental of or services;
– viewers must be clearly informed of the existence of a sponsorship agreement. Sponsored programmes must be clearly identified as such by the surname (name), logo and/or any other symbol of the sponsor such as a reference to his product(s) or service(s) or a distinctive sign thereof in an appropriate way at the beginning, during and/or at the end of the programmes.

- Audiovisual media services, radio programmes and/or parts thereof may not be sponsored by persons whose principal activity is the manufacture or sale of cigarettes and other tobacco products.
- Where audiovisual media services, radio programmes and/or individual programmes are sponsored by persons whose activities include the manufacture or sale of medicinal products or medical treatment, they may promote the name (logo) or any other image of the sponsor but must not promote specific medicinal products or medical treatments available only on prescription.
- News programmes may not be sponsored.

§5. Product Placement

285. By the law of 2010, LPIP was supplemented with Article 40^1 which allowed product placement in programmes, except for children's programmes and news programmes.

286. Now the article sets out that product placement is allowed in cinematographic works, films and series made for audiovisual media services, sports programmes and entertainment programmes. Product placement is also allowed where, without payment agreed upon between persons, certain goods or services, such as prizes or other goods or services necessary to produce a programme, are included in the programme (Article 40^1(1)).

287. Article 40^1(2) sets out requirements for product placement which shall be applied cumulatively:

- the content and scheduling of programmes and the editorial responsibility and independence of the media service provider may in no circumstances be influenced;
- they may not directly encourage the purchase or rental of goods or services;
- they may not give undue prominence to the product in question;
- viewers must be clearly informed of the existence of product placement. Programmes containing product placement must be appropriately identified at the start and the end of the programme and when a programme resumes after an advertising break in order to avoid any confusion on the part of the viewer.

288. The following product placement is prohibited (Article 40^1(3)):

- tobacco products or product placement from undertakings whose principal activity is the manufacture or sale of tobacco products;
- medical treatments or medicinal products available only on prescription.

Chapter 6. Right to Information

§1. Access to Major Events

289. A list of events considered to be of major importance for society in the Republic of Lithuania[187] is drawn up by the Commission and approved by the Government (Article 38(7) of LPIP).

290. Article 38(6) of LPIP sets out the requirements for the broadcast of programmes covering major events. Broadcasters of television programmes under the jurisdiction of the Republic of Lithuania who have acquired the exclusive rights to broadcast programmes covering the events of major importance for society taking place in Lithuania or outside its territory must broadcast the events of major importance for society live or on a deferred basis only in uncoded and free of charge national television programmes which are transmitted by television networks of any technological form and received in the territory populated by more than 60 per cent of the residents of the Republic of Lithuania. Deferred broadcasts of the events of major importance to society must be shown not later than 24 hours after the end of an event of major importance for society. If a television broadcaster may not guarantee the conditions laid above in this paragraph must, within a reasonable time before the event of major importance for society, take all measures to transfer the said rights to another television broadcaster. Broadcasters of television programmes under the jurisdiction of the Republic of Lithuania may not exercise the exclusive rights to broadcast programmes intended to cover events of major importance for society taking place in Lithuania or outside its territory in such a way as to deprive a substantial proportion of people residing in another Member State of the European Union, a state of the European Economic Area or a state which has ratified the Council of Europe Convention on Transfrontier Television of the possibility of following the events taking place in Lithuania or outside its territory which, under the legal acts of that state, are designated as events of major importance for society.

291. Article 12 of LPIP regulates the accreditation of journalists. Article 12(1) sets out that a producer and/or disseminator of public information shall have the right to accredit their journalists with state institutions, political parties, political organizations and associations as well as with other institutions by agreement between the parties. Article 12(2) indicates that a journalist may take part in the meetings and other events of the institution or organization he has been accredited with; they shall be provided with verbatim reports, minutes and other documents or copies thereof subject to conditions established by mutual agreement. Article 12(3)

187. For example, the Summer and Winter Olympic Games (opening and closing ceremonies, competitions involving Lithuanian athletes), basketball matches played by the Lithuanian national men's basketball team, the Lithuanian Song Festival, etc. (Resolution No. 288 of the Government of the Republic of Lithuania of 3 Apr. 2013 'On Approval of the List of Events Significant to the Society of the Republic of Lithuania'.

indicates that foreign journalists accredited with the Ministry of Foreign Affairs of the Republic of Lithuania shall have the same rights to collect and publish information as Lithuanian journalists.

§2. Short News Reporting

292. Both the public broadcaster and the commercial broadcasters are granted the right to prepare up to ninety-second segments of all national and foreign political, cultural, sports or other events, regardless of who has exclusive rights to this event broadcast (Article 5(3) of the LNRT and Article 38(1) of LPIP).

293. LPIP further specifies that short news reports must be broadcast not earlier than after the end of the live broadcast of the event of public importance. Broadcasters of television programmes shall not pay for the broadcasting of short news reports to the broadcasters of television programmes who have acquired exclusive rights for the provision of information covering the event of major importance to society, except for the cases where the provision of access to events of major importance for society entails additional costs on the part of the broadcaster of television programmes who provide such access. The payment for the provision of access to events of major importance for society may not exceed the additional costs directly incurred in providing access.

294. All broadcasters of television programmes established in any Member State of the European Union or a state of the European Economic Area wishing to produce short news reports shall have the right to access on a fair, reasonable and non-discriminatory basis to events of major importance to society which are transmitted on an exclusive basis by the audiovisual media service provider under the jurisdiction of the Republic of Lithuania.

295. Short news reports may be used solely for general news programmes and may be used in on-demand audiovisual media services only if the same programme is offered on a deferred basis by the same audiovisual media service provider.

Chapter 7. Access to Networks

§1. Must Carry Rules

296. LEC[188] implements European Union Directives regulating must-carry rules of operators.

297. The European Union's open Internet access policy guarantees the service user the right to access all lawful content on the Internet and to distribute his content regardless of the Internet access provider chosen, the applications used or how the information is disseminated.

298. The CRA shall closely monitor and ensure compliance with the provisions of Regulation (EU) 2015/2120, establishing a policy on open Internet access and shall aim to ensure continuous and non-discriminatory access to Internet access of a quality commensurate with technological developments. This principle of net neutrality states that all Internet users have equal access and connection speed rights – it is forbidden to block or slow down the user's Internet traffic; it is mandatory to treat all traffic equally, regardless of the type or content of the traffic, Article 3.

188. Official Gazette 2004, No. 69-2382, code 1041010ISTA0IX-2135.

Chapter 8. Standards and Interoperability

299. Article 24 of the LEC indicates that providers of electronic communications networks used for the distribution of digital television services shall ensure the possibility to distribute wide-screen digital television services and programmes. Operators that receive and redistribute wide-screen digital television services or programmes shall maintain that wide-screen format.

300. Article 25(1) of the same law sets out that undertakings controlling conditional access systems shall use only such systems of conditional access to digital radio and/or television services, irrespective of the means of transmission, that would have the necessary technical capability for cost-effective transmission control (i.e. technical procedures enabling to transfer conditional access control from one broadcaster (transmission provider) to another broadcaster (transmission provider), allowing the possibility for full control at a local or regional level of the services by operators using such systems. Part 2 of the same article indicates that undertakings that provide conditional access services to digital radio and/or television services, irrespective of the means of transmission, whose services broadcasters depend on to reach any group of potential viewers or listeners, irrespective of the means of transmission, must:

- offer to all broadcasters, on a fair, reasonable and non-discriminatory basis, technical services enabling the broadcasters' digitally transmitted services to be received by viewers or listeners authorized by means of decoders provided and administered by the service providers (operators);
- if undertakings are engaged, apart from the provision of conditional access to digital radio and/or television services, in other activities, keep separate financial accounts regarding their activity as conditional access providers in accordance with the rules for accounting separation laid down by the CRA and in conformity with requirements related to accounting separation, including the auditing requirement.

Part IV. Cross-Ownership Regulation

301. The Republic of Lithuania seeks to create conditions for effective competition and its development in the field of electronic communications as well as conditions to prevent the abuse of market power by undertakings (Article 14 of the LEC). The Competition Council is in charge of supervision of competition in the field of electronic communications in accordance with the Law on Competition.

302. According to Article 15 of the LEC, an undertaking shall be considered to have significant market power if, either individually or jointly with others, it enjoys a position equivalent to dominance, i.e. a position of economic strength affording it a power to behave to an appreciable extent independently of competitors, customers and ultimately consumers. Where an undertaking has significant market power on the relevant market, it may also be considered to have significant market power on a closely related market, if the links between the two markets are such as to allow the market power held in one market to be leveraged into the other market, thereby strengthening the market power of the undertaking. An undertaking shall be identified as having significant market power where this has been determined by a decision of the CRA based on market analysis, and it shall be deemed as such until the CRA determines by its decision based on another market analysis that the undertaking does not have significant market power.

303. The CRA has the right to impose the following obligations on undertakings having significant market power on the relevant market:

- obligation of transparency;
- obligation of non-discrimination;
- obligation of accounting separation;
- obligation to provide access;
- obligations of price control and cost accounting;
- obligation of functional separation;
- obligations concerning the provision of services to end-users.

Part V. Supervision: Media Regulator

Chapter 1. Organization

304. LEC regulates how the media portrays and distributes certain public opinion. Article 4(2) sets out that electronic communications activities in the Republic of Lithuania shall be regulated by the CRA and other state institutions.

305. Although funded from the State budget, the CRA is an independent state institution responsible for the regulation of electronic communications activities and for the supervision of compliance with and implementation of the provisions of the LEC, except where such supervision and implementation fall within the scope of competence of other state institutions. The CRA is a public legal entity and is financed from the state budget and a separate budget of its own, comprised of revenues from services provided and work performed.

Chapter 2. Tasks

306. The objective of the CRA is to develop effective competition in the field of electronic communications, efficient use of electronic communications resources and ensured protection of the rights of consumers of electronic communications services (Article 8(1) of the LEC).

307. The main tasks of the CRA are the following (Article 8(2) of the LEC):

(1) to ensure the conditions necessary for effective competition and non-discrimination in the markets of electronic communications;
(2) to promote the expansion and development of electronic communications infrastructure;
(3) to ensure protection of the rights and legitimate interests of the users of electronic communications services, including the disabled, elderly and users of special social needs;
(4) to promote effective long-term investments and innovation implementation, as well as the development of electronic communications;
(5) to ensure an effective use of electronic communications resources and sufficient national telephone numbering resources necessary for provision of public electronic communications services;
(6) to ensure that the equipment and devices used in the Republic of Lithuania are in conformity with the mandatory requirements in force in the Republic of Lithuania and ensure the electromagnetic compatibility of the equipment and devices;
(7) etc.

Chapter 3. Sanctioning Powers

308. If the CRA finds that an undertaking does not comply with the legal acts specifying the terms and conditions for engaging in electronic communications activities or the terms and conditions for the use of electronic communications resources or fails to fulfil one or more of the obligations imposed on it as an undertaking having significant market power on the relevant market or designated to provide universal service, or does not fulfil the obligations imposed by the CRA, it shall notify the undertaking in writing of the infringements identified and give the undertaking an opportunity to present its views within a reasonable time limit set by the CRA.

309. The CRA has the right to require to bring the infringement referred to above to an end immediately or within a reasonable time limit set by the CRA or take other corresponding and proportionate measures to ensure enforcement of legal acts, including the imposition set out in Article 74 of the LEC.

310. Also, as mentioned before, they can advise LRTK to revoke or put on hold the licensee or LRT (paragraph 189).

Selected Bibliography

Markauskas, L. 'Reklamos teisinis reglamentavimas: teorija ir praktika' ['Regulation of Advertising: Theory and Practice'], edited by Vilnius: Mokesčių srautas, 2008.

Matačinskaitė, J. 'Žurnalisto kompetencijos ir gebėjimai šiandienos žiniasklaidoje' [Journalist's Competences and Skills in Modern Media']. *Mokslo darbų žurnalas (Komunikacija ir informacija)* 3 (2010).

Meškauskaitė, L. 'Žiniasklaidos teisė', 2-asis leidimas [*Media Law*, 2nd ed.], Vilnius: Registrų centras, 2018.

Šindeikis, A. 'Žodžio laisvė ir jos ribų kaita per du atkurtos nepriklausomybės dešimtmečius' ['Freedom of Speech and Its Limits During Two Decades of Independence']. *Jurisprudencija* 20(3) (2013).

Žiliukaitė R., Poviliūnas A., Savicka A., *Lietuvos visuomenės vertybių kaita per dvidešimt nepriklausomybės metų:* Monografija 2016.

Selected Bibliography

Index

The numbers here refer to the paragraph numbers.

Index

www.ingramcontent.com/pod-product-compliance
Lightning Source LLC
Chambersburg PA
CBHW071355230926
51846CB00002B/558
9789403549958